piano · vocal · guitar

newsboys

ISBN 978-1-4234-5548-6

HAL•LEONARD®
CORPORATION

7777 W. BLUEMOUND RD. P.O. BOX 13819 MILWAUKEE, WI 53213

Visit Hal Leonard Online at
www.halleonard.com

I FOUGHT THE LA...

Words and Music by TED TJORNHOM,
STEVE TAYLOR and PETER FURLER

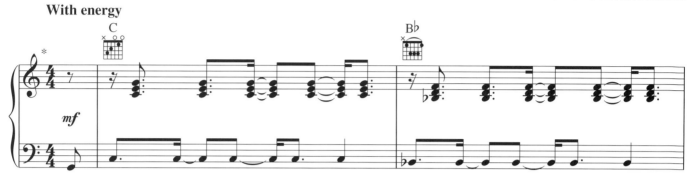

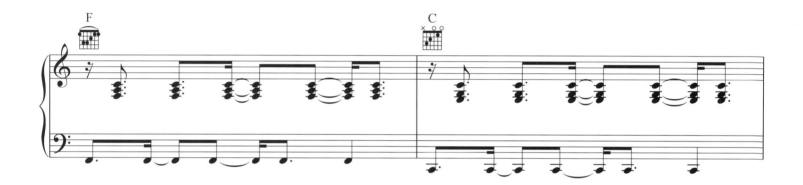

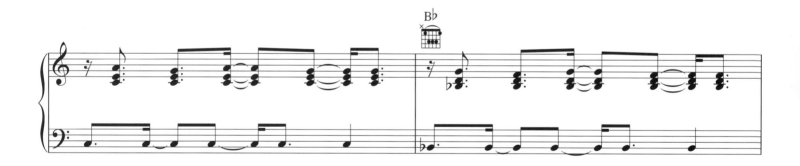

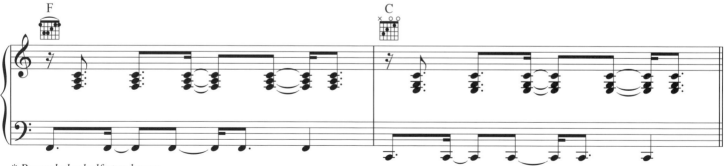

Recorded a half step lower.

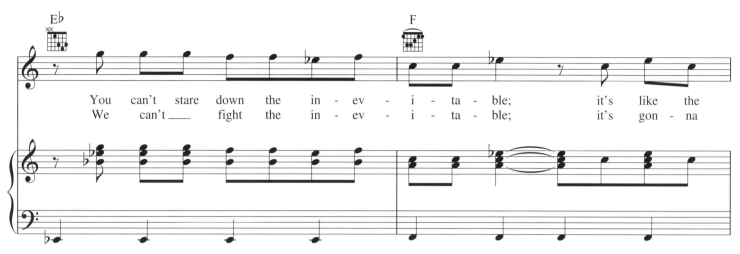

Eb · F

You can't stare down the in - ev - i - ta - ble; it's like the
We can't ___ fight the in - ev - i - ta - ble; it's gon - na

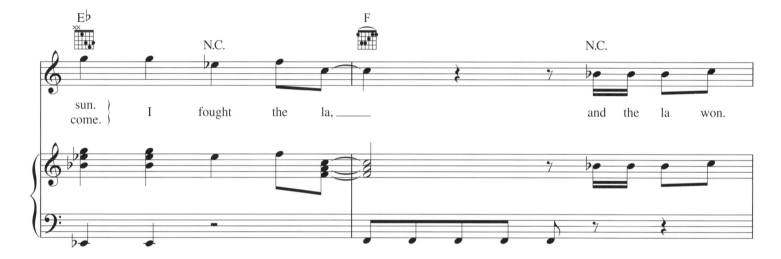

Eb · N.C. · F · N.C.

sun. } I fought the la, ___ and the la won.
come. }

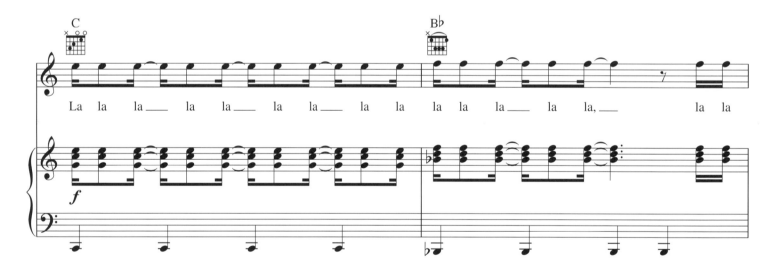

C · Bb

La la la ___ la la ___ la la ___ la la la la la ___ la la, ___ la la

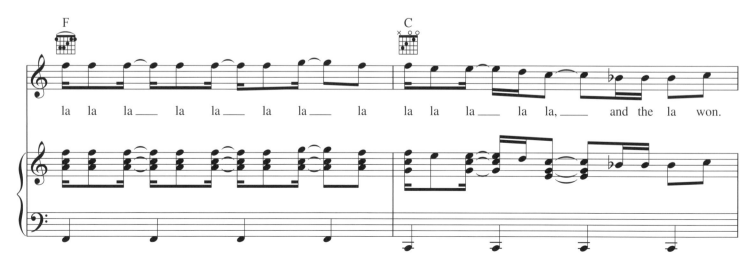

F · C

la la la ___ la la ___ la la ___ la la la la ___ la la, ___ and the la won.

La la la la la la la la la la la la la la, la la

la la la la la la la la la la la la la.

la la la la la. Ah,

ah.

It's in-ev-i-ta-

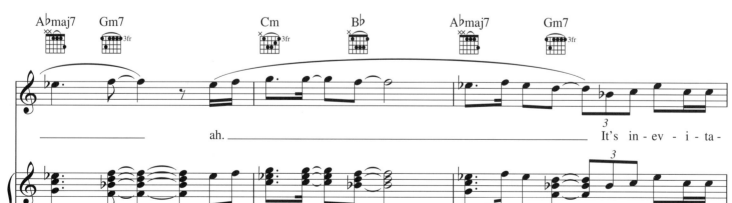

ble.

You can't fight the in - ev - i - ta - ble. ___

La la la ___ la la ___ la la la la

la la la ___ la la, ___ la la la la la ___ la la la ___ la

la la la la la la, yeah, the la won. La la la la la la la la la

la la la la la, la la la la la la la la la la

1, 2
la la la la la., and the la won.

3
la la la la la.

BREAKFAST

Words and Music by PETER FURLER
and STEVE TAYLOR

Rock beat

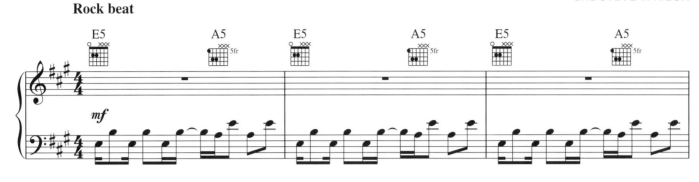

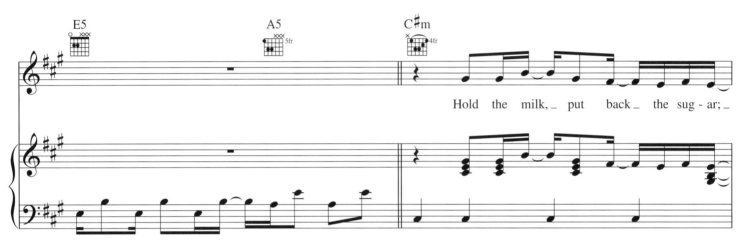

Hold the milk, __ put back __ the sug-ar; __ they are pow'r-less to __ con-sole.

We've gath-ered here __ to sprin - kle ash-

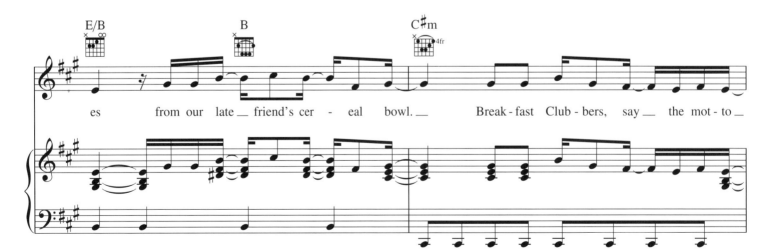

es from our late __ friend's cer - eal bowl. __ Break-fast Club-bers, say __ the mot-to

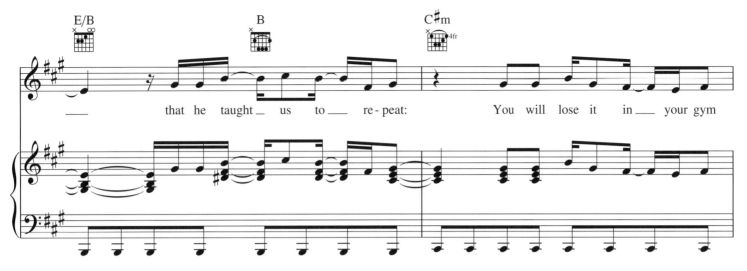

that he taught __ us to __ re - peat: You will lose it in __ your gym

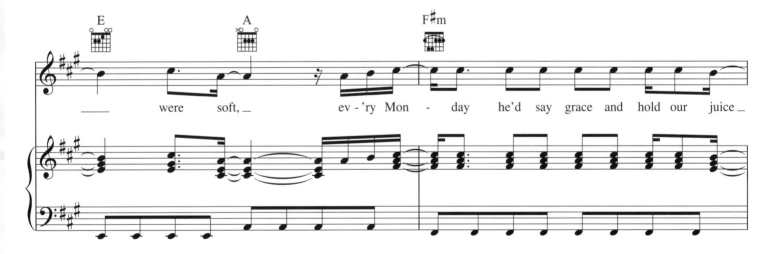

class if you wait __ till noon __ to eat. Back when the Chess __ Club said our eggs __

__ were soft, __ ev - 'ry Mon - day he'd say grace and hold our juice __

__ a - loft. __ Oh, none of us knew his check - out time __ would

come so soon, __ but be - fore __ his brain stopped wav - ing, he __ com - posed __

__ this tune: __ When the toast is __ burned __ and all the

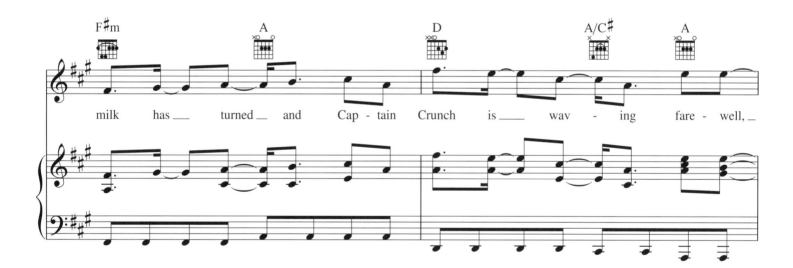

milk has __ turned __ and Cap - tain Crunch is __ wav - ing fare - well, __

__ when the Big One __ finds __ you, may this

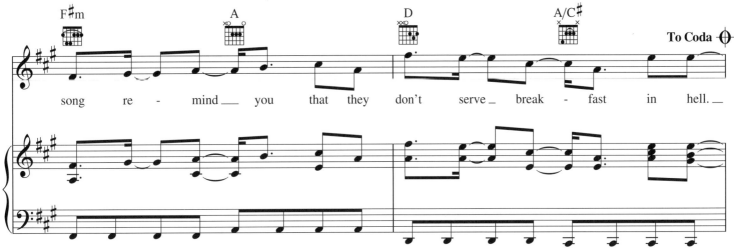

To Coda

song re - mind __ you that they don't serve __ break - fast in hell. __

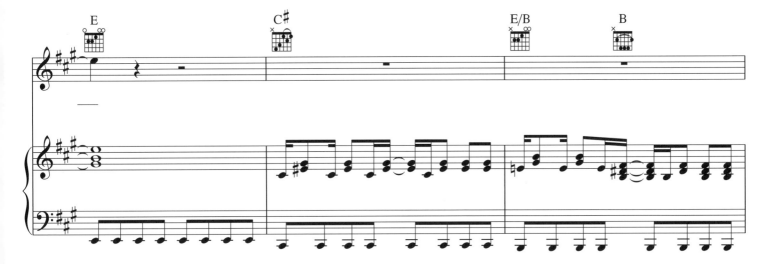

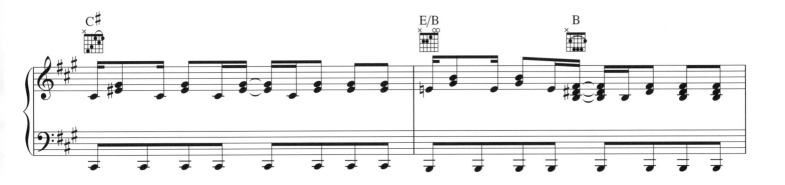

Break - fast Club - bers, drop __ the hank - ies. Though to some __ our friend __ was odd,

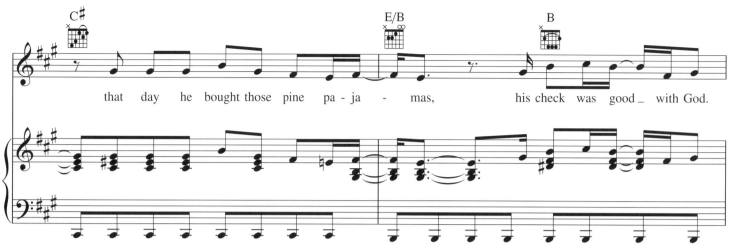

that day he bought those pine pa-ja-mas, his check was good __ with God.

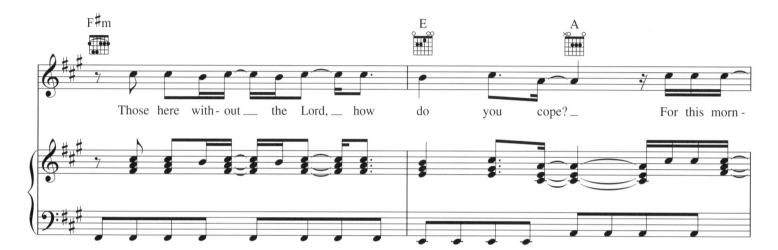

Those here with-out __ the Lord, __ how do you cope? __ For this morn-

-ing we don't mourn __ like those who have __ no hope. __ Oh,

rise up, Froot Loop lov-ers, sing __ out sweet and low. __ With

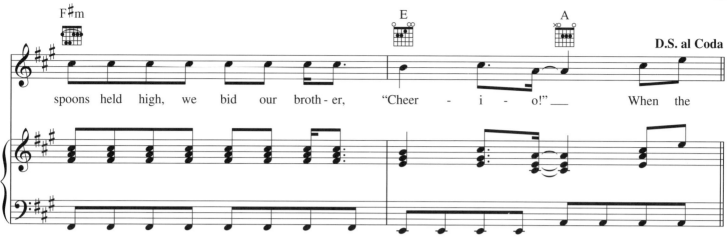

D.S. al Coda

spoons held high, we bid our broth - er, "Cheer - i - o!" ___ When the

CODA

Whistle (2nd time only)

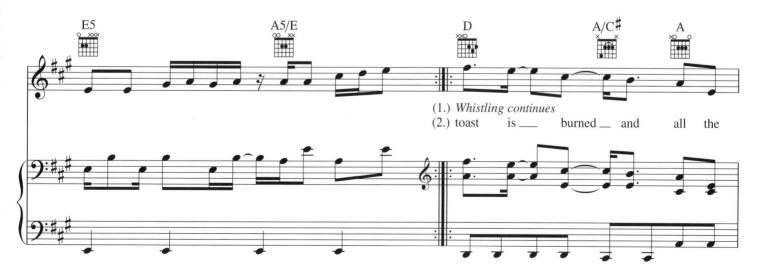

(1.) *Whistling continues*
(2.) toast is ___ burned ___ and all the

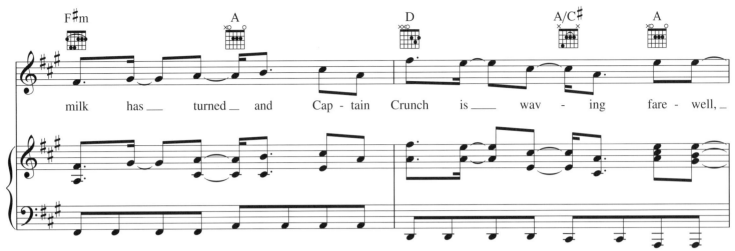

milk has __ turned __ and Cap - tain Crunch is __ wav - ing fare - well, __

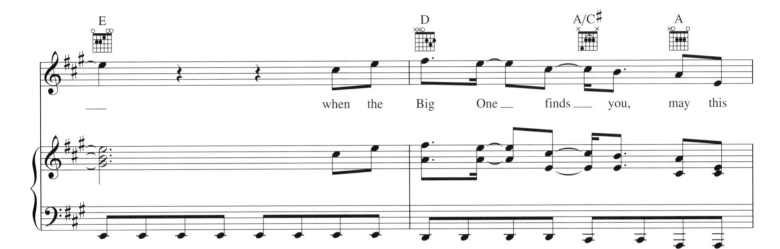

__ when the Big One __ finds __ you, may this

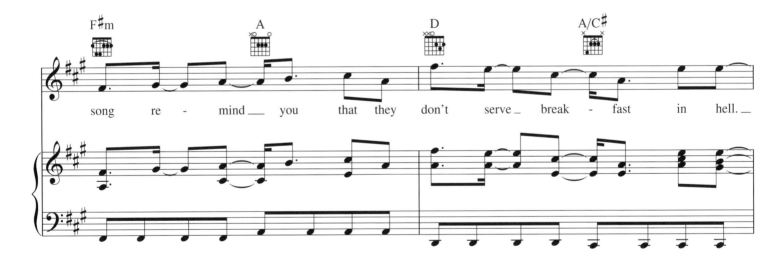

song re - mind __ you that they don't serve __ break - fast in hell. __

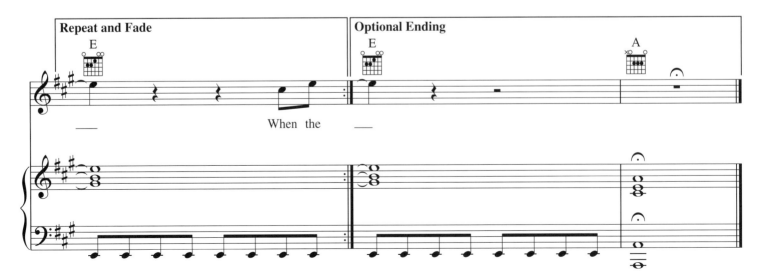

Repeat and Fade

Optional Ending

__ When the __

IN THE BELLY OF THE WHALE

Words by STEVE TAYLOR
Music by PETER FURLER

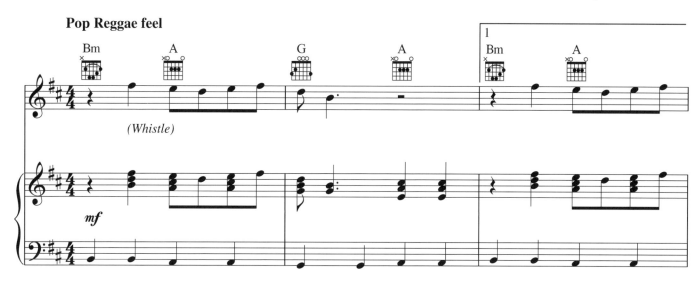

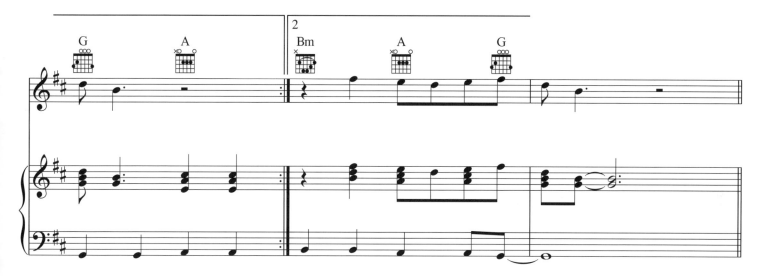

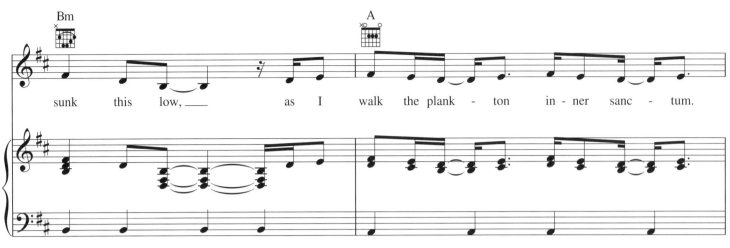

sunk this low, ___ as I walk the plank - ton in - ner sanc - tum.

Got out - ta Dodge, _ sailed on a "bon - less" bon _ voy - age. __ You said, "North," _

___ I head - ed south, _ tossed o - ver - board. __ Good Lord, that's a real - ly large __ mouth. _

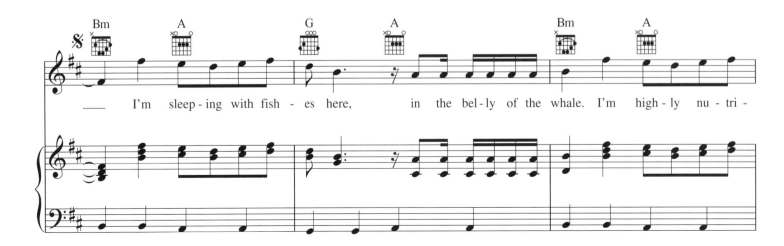

___ I'm sleep - ing with fish - es here, in the bel - ly of the whale. I'm high - ly nu - tri -

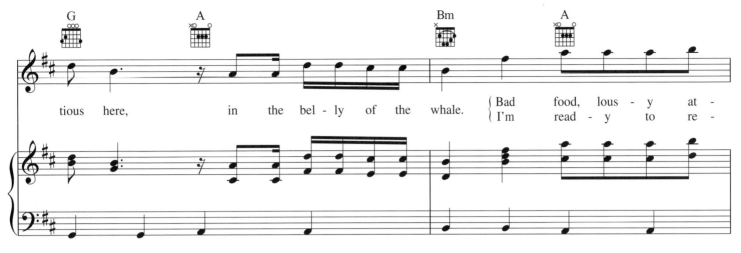

tious here, in the bel-ly of the whale. { Bad food, lous-y at-
{ I'm read-y to re-

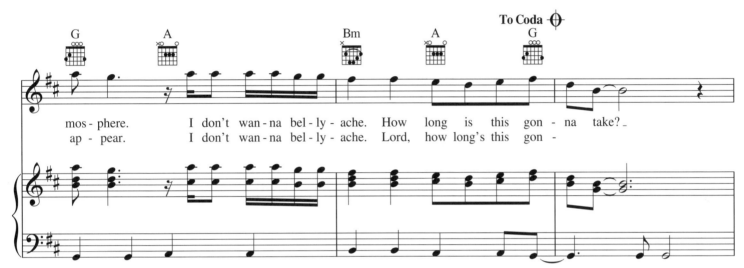

mos-phere. I don't wan-na bel-ly-ache. How long is this gon-na take?
ap-pear. I don't wan-na bel-ly-ache. Lord, how long's this gon-

To Coda ⊕

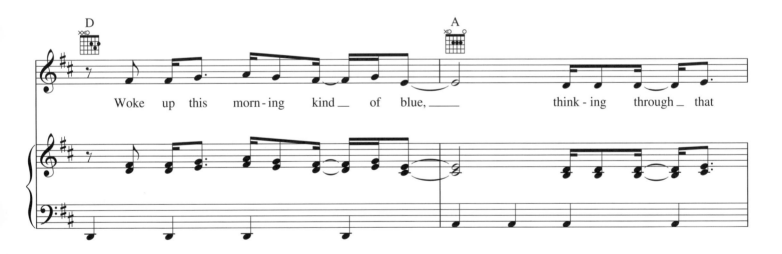

Woke up this morn-ing kind of blue, think-ing through that

age-old ques-tion, how to ex-it a whale's di-ges-tion.

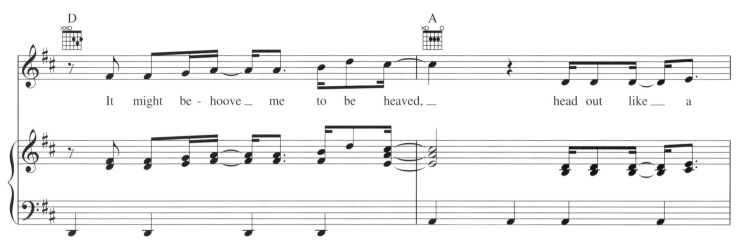

It might be-hoove_ me to be heaved,_ head out like_ a

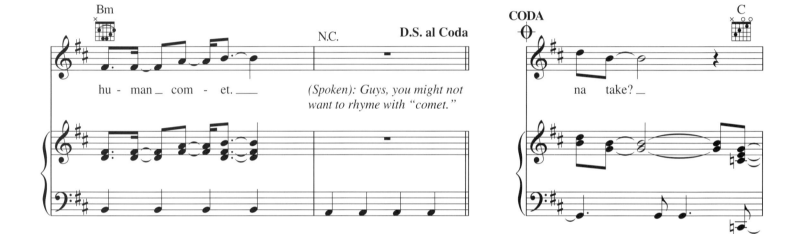

hu - man_ com - et. _

(Spoken): Guys, you might not want to rhyme with "comet."

D.S. al Coda

CODA

na take? _

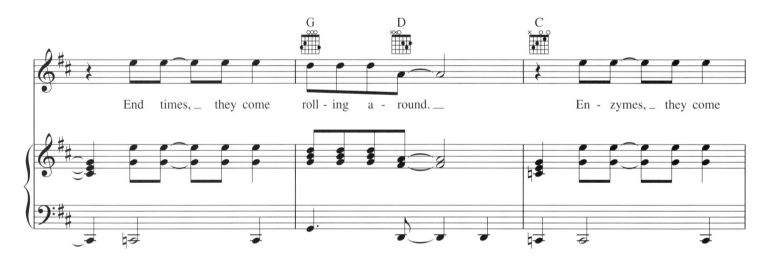

End times, _ they come roll - ing a - round. _ En - zymes, _ they come

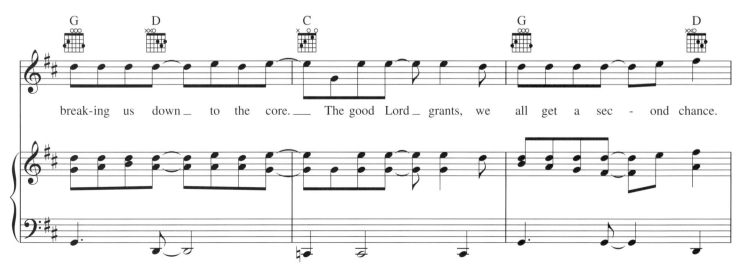

break-ing us down_ to the core._ The good Lord_ grants, we all get a sec - ond chance.

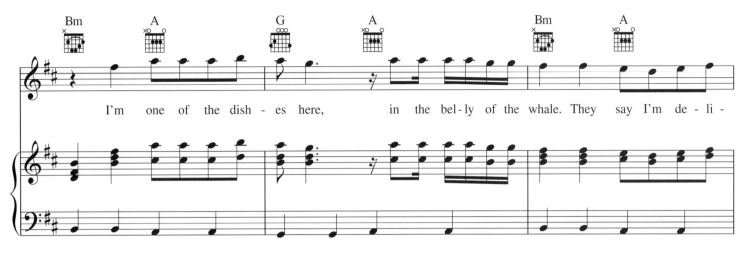

I'm one of the dish - es here, in the bel - ly of the whale. They say I'm de - li -

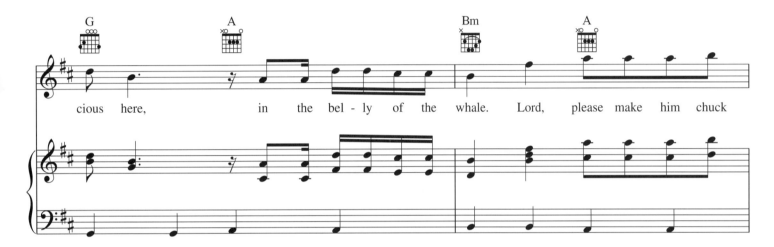

cious here, in the bel - ly of the whale. Lord, please make him chuck

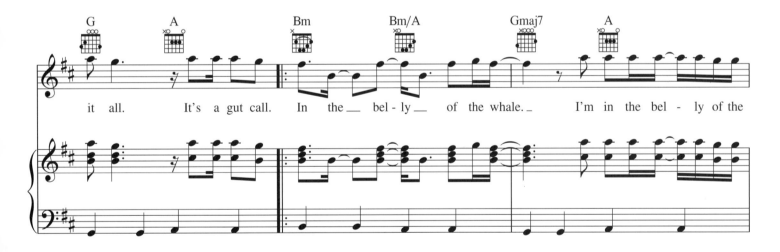

it all. It's a gut call. In the __ bel - ly __ of the whale. __ I'm in the bel - ly of the

Repeat ad lib. and Fade

Optional Ending

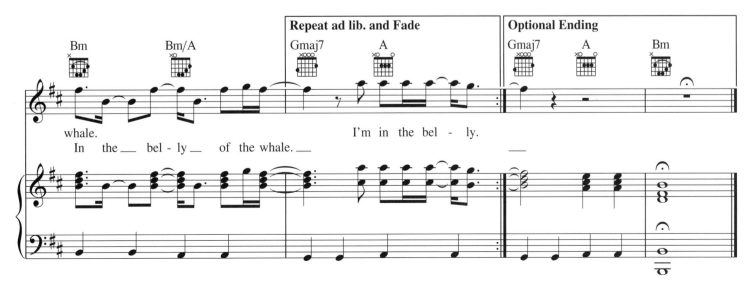

whale. I'm in the bel - ly.

In the __ bel - ly __ of the whale. __

MILLION PIECES

Words and Music by PETER FURLER
and STEVE TAYLOR

Moderately slow

(Doot doo doo doot.) Oh yeah. (Doot doo doo doot.) Oh

yeah. (Doot doo doo doot.) Oh yeah. _____ (Doot doo doo doot.) Oh, they

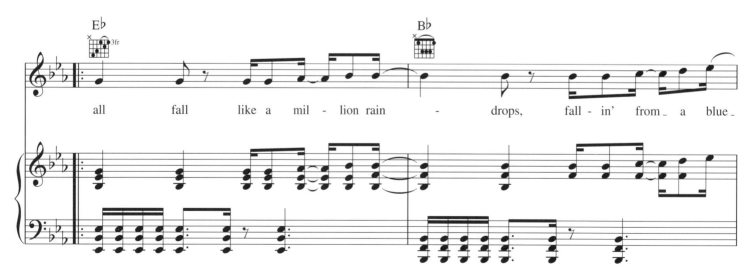

all fall like a mil-lion rain - drops, fall-in' from a blue

* Recorded a half step higher.

sky, kiss-in' your cares_ good-bye._ Oh,_ as they

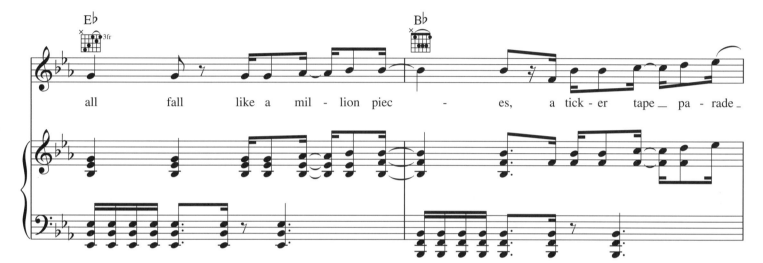

all fall like a mil-lion piec - es, a tick-er tape_ pa-rade_

high, and now you're free_ to fly._

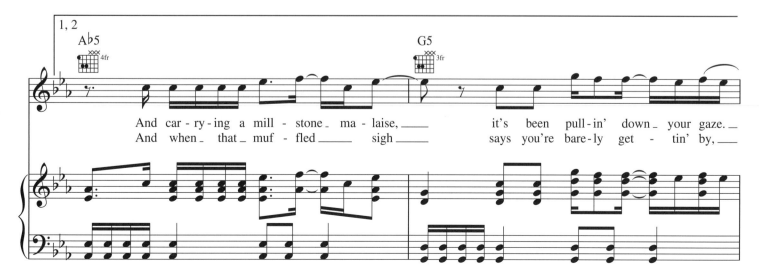

And car-ry-ing a mill-stone ma-laise,_ it's been pull-in' down_ your gaze._
And when_ that_ muf-fled_ sigh_ says you're bare-ly get-tin' by,_

It's time to leave your bur - dens in a pyre; __ set a bon - fire, __

__ 'cause when you lay your bur - dens down, __ when you drop them bur - dens,

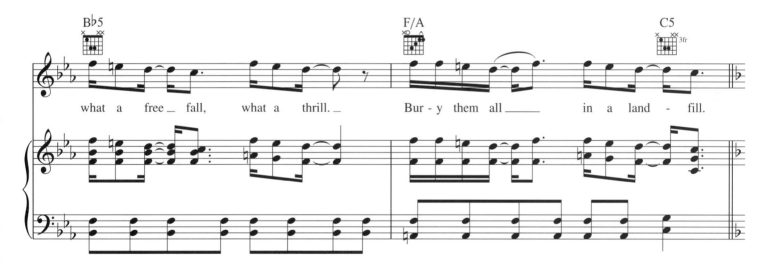

what a free __ fall, what a thrill. __ Bur - y them all _____ in a land - fill.

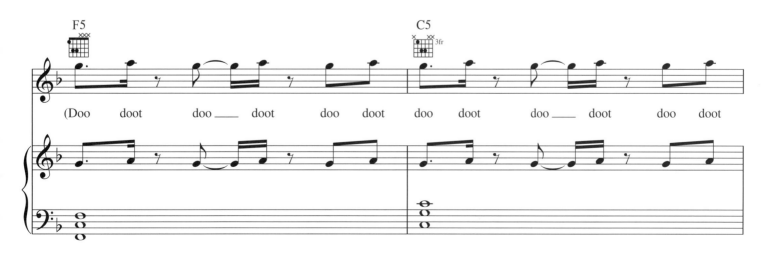

(Doo doot doo __ doot doo doot doo doot doo __ doot doo doot

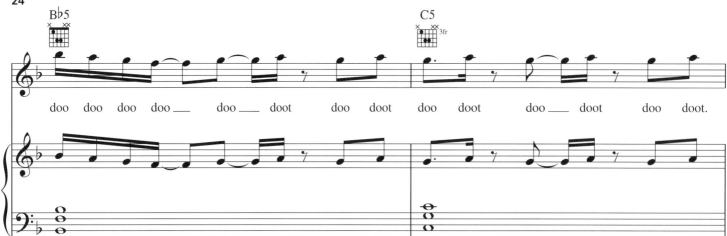

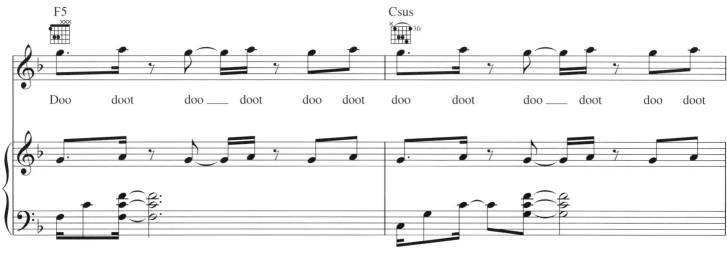

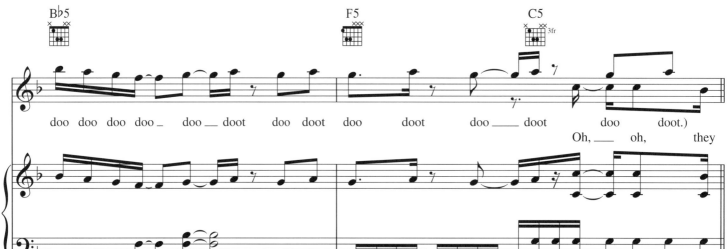

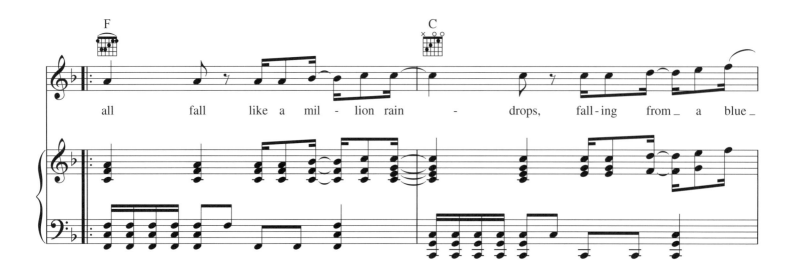

SHINE

Words and Music by PETER FURLER
and STEVE TAYLOR

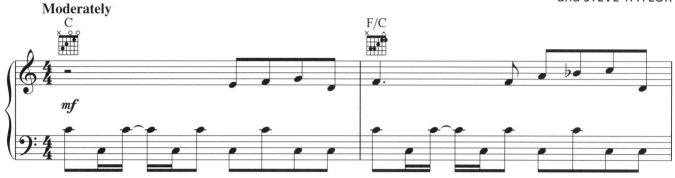

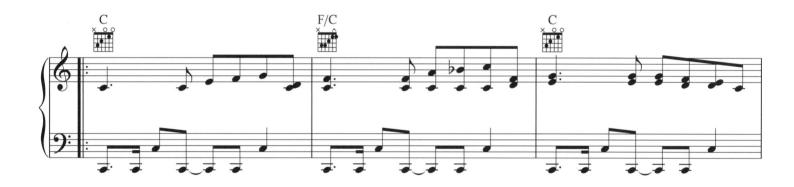

Dull as dirt,___ you can't as - sert the kind of light___
Out of the shak - er and on - to the plate, it is - n't Kar -

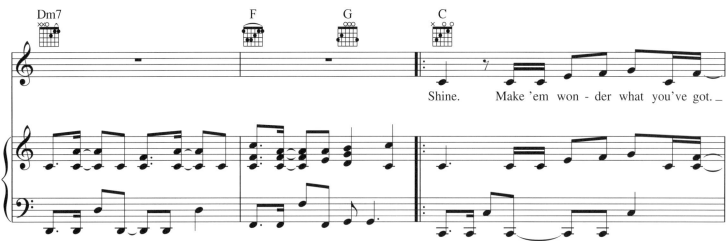

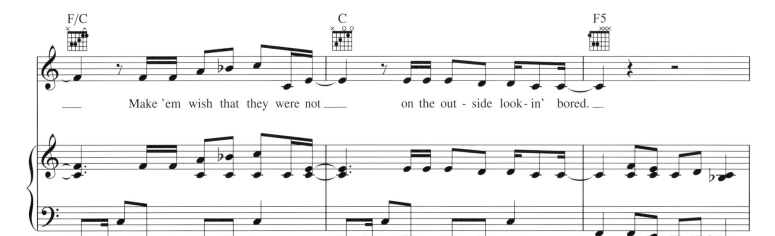

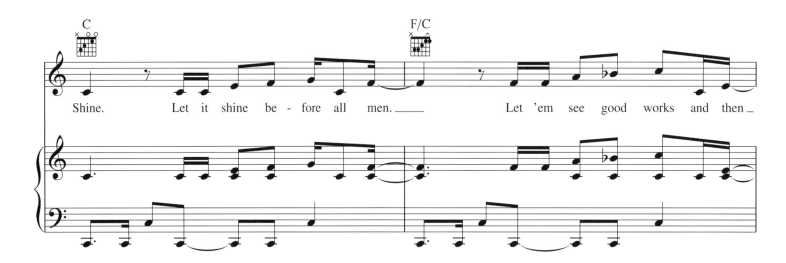

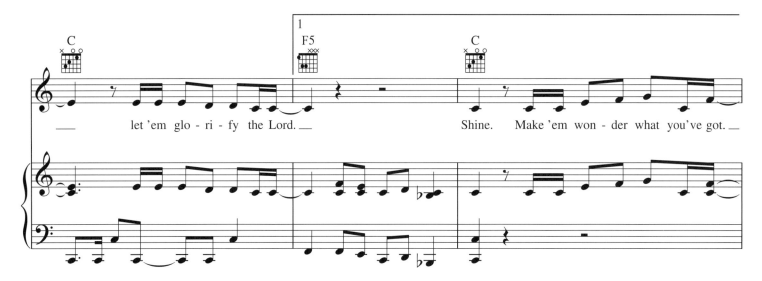

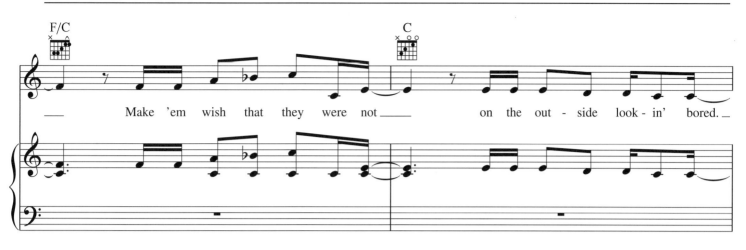

Make 'em wish that they were not _____ on the out-side look-in' bored. _

_ Shine. Let it shine be-fore all men. _

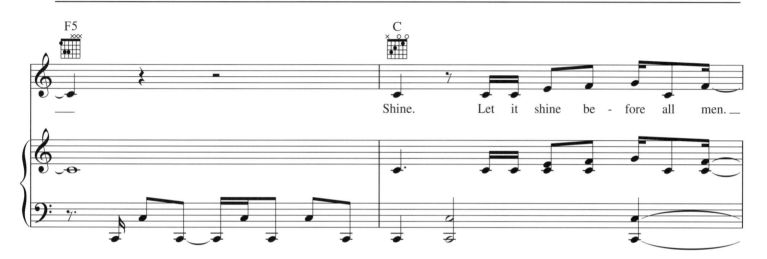

_ Let 'em see good works and then _____ let 'em glo-ri-fy the Lord. _

Shine.

SOMETHING BEAUTIFUL

Words and Music by
PETER FURLER

With a driving beat

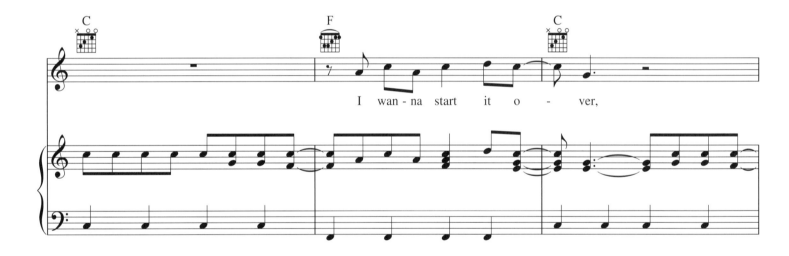

I wan-na start it o-ver,

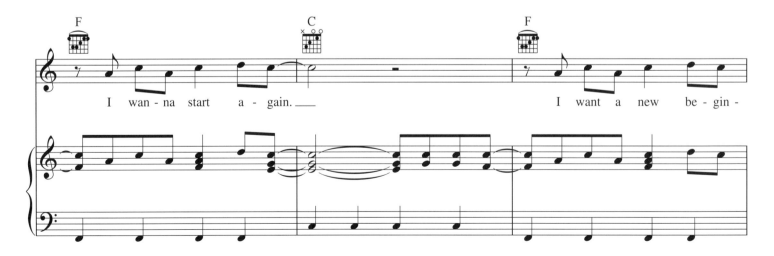

I wan-na start a-gain. ___ I want a new be-gin-

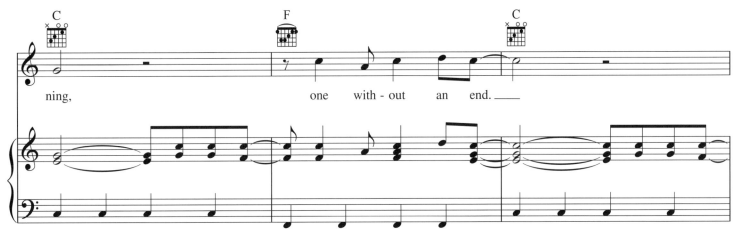

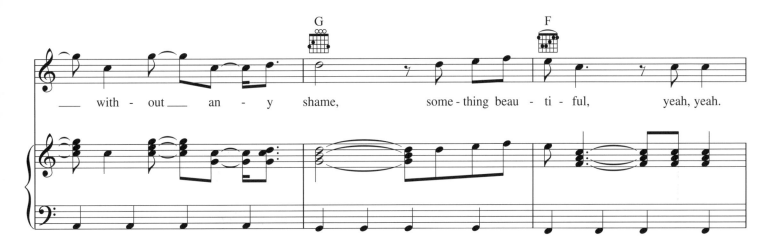

Like a song ___ that stirs ___ in ___ my head sing - ing, "Love ___

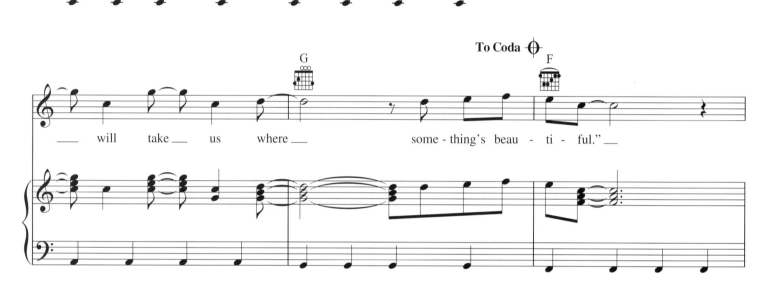

___ will take ___ us where ___ some - thing's beau - ti - ful." ___

I've heard it in the si - lence,

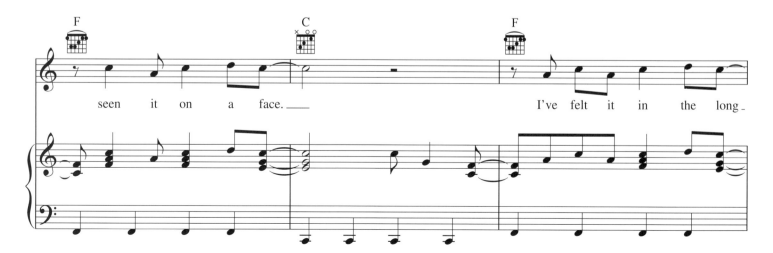

seen it on a face. ___ I've felt it in the long ___

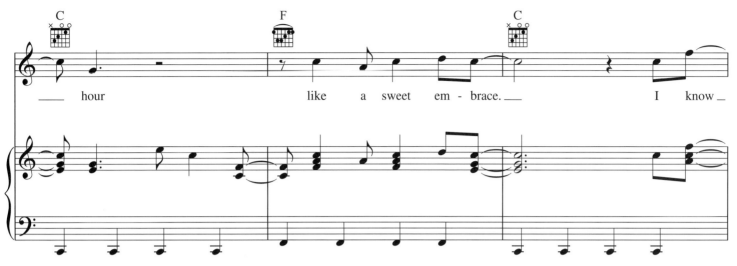

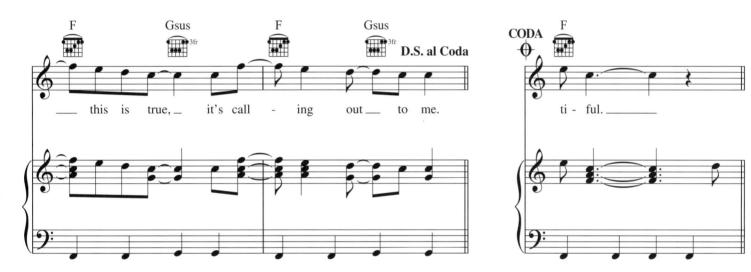

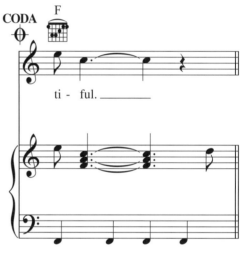

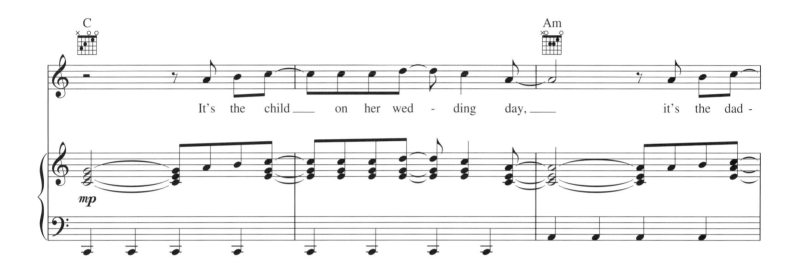

It's the child ___ on her wed - ding day, ___ it's the dad -

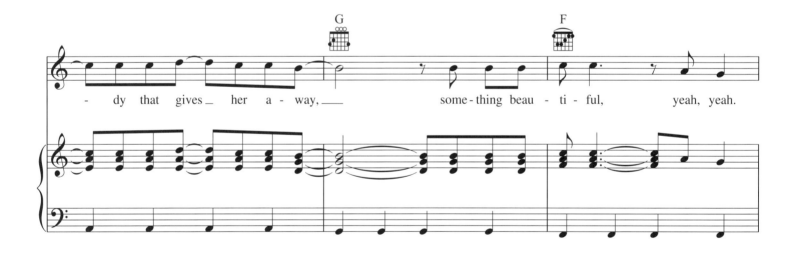

- dy that gives ___ her a - way, ___ some - thing beau - ti - ful, ___ yeah, yeah.

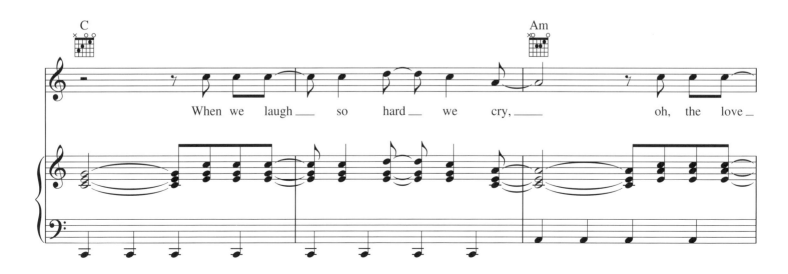

When we laugh ___ so hard ___ we cry, ___ oh, the love ___

be - tween _ you and I, _____ some-thing beau - ti - ful. __

It's a voice ___ that whis - pers ___ my name, it's a kiss __

__ with - out ___ an - y shame, some-thing beau - ti - ful, yeah, yeah.

Like a song ___ that stirs ___ in ___ my head sing - ing, "Love __

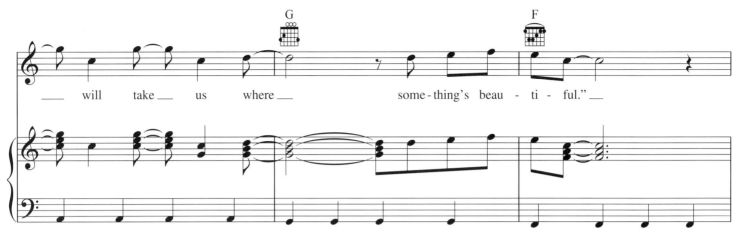

____ will take ___ us where ___ some-thing's beau - ti - ful."___

It's the child ___ on her wed - ding day, ___ it's the dad-

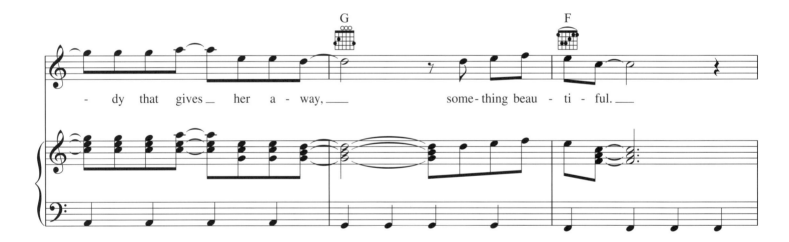

- dy that gives ___ her a - way, ___ some-thing beau - ti - ful. ___

When we laugh ___ so hard ___ we cry, ___ it's the love ___

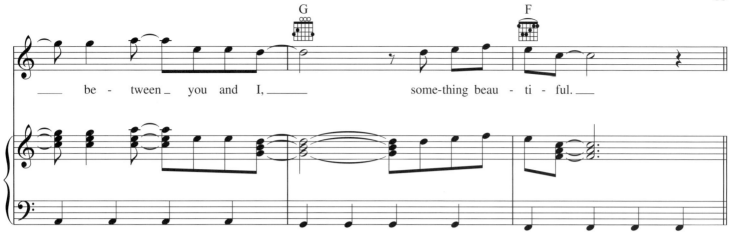

be - tween_ you and I,_____ some-thing beau - ti - ful._

ti - ful. ___

Some - thing beau -

HE REIGNS

Words and Music by PETER FURLER
and STEVE TAYLOR

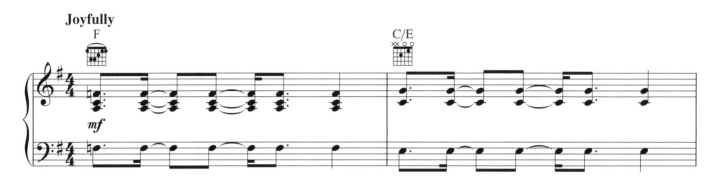

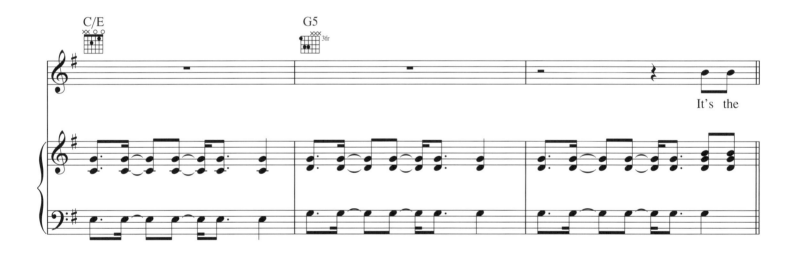

It's the

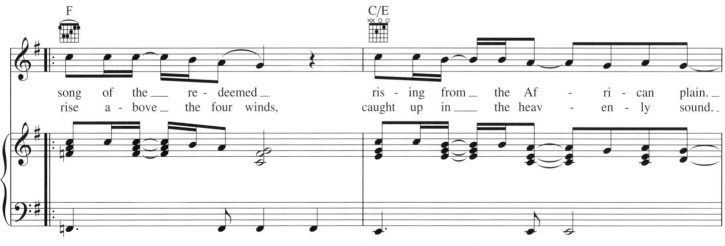

song of the __ re - deemed __ rising from __ the Af - ri - can plain. __
rise a - bove __ the four winds, caught up in __ the heav - en - ly sound. __

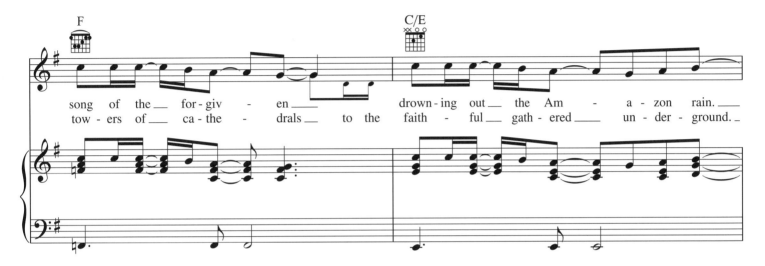

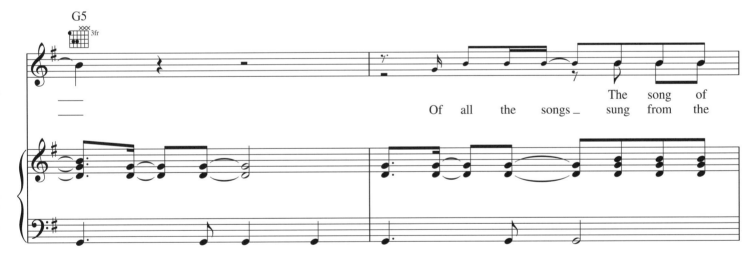

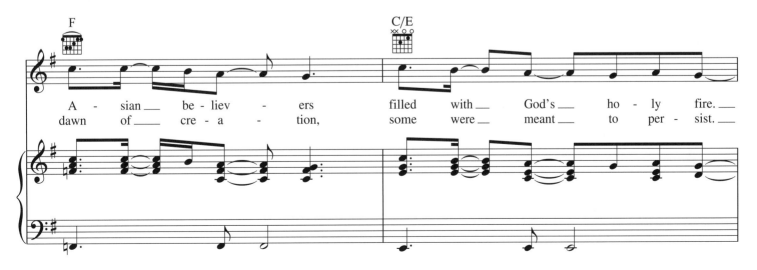

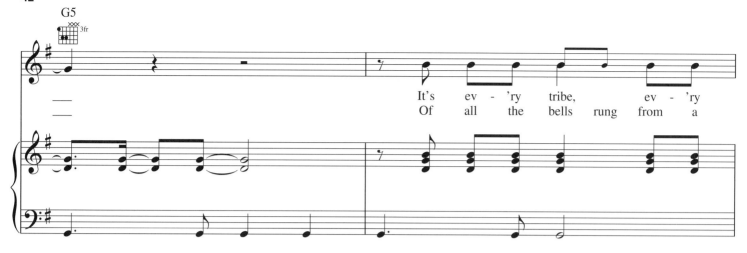

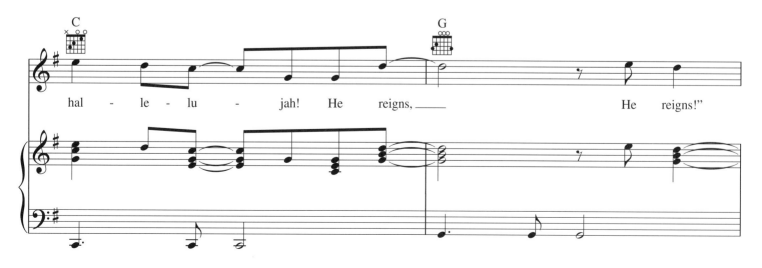

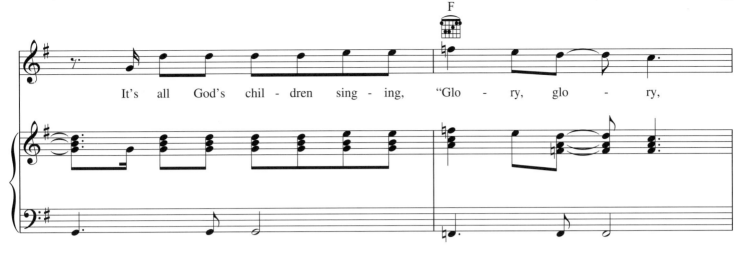

It's all God's chil-dren sing-ing, "Glo-ry, glo-ry,

hal-le-lu-jah! He reigns, ___ He reigns." Let it

It's all God's chil-dren sing-ing, "Glo-ry, glo-ry,

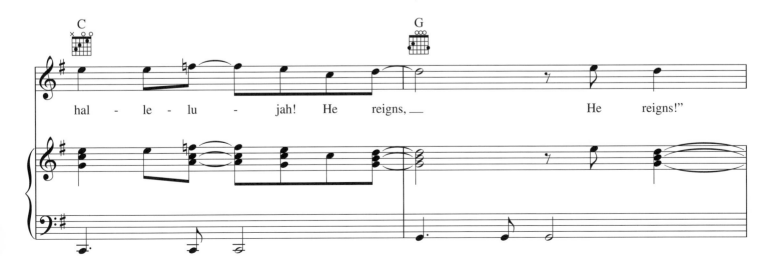

hal-le-lu-jah! He reigns, ___ He reigns!"

It's all God's chil - dren sing - ing, "Glo - ry, glo - ry,

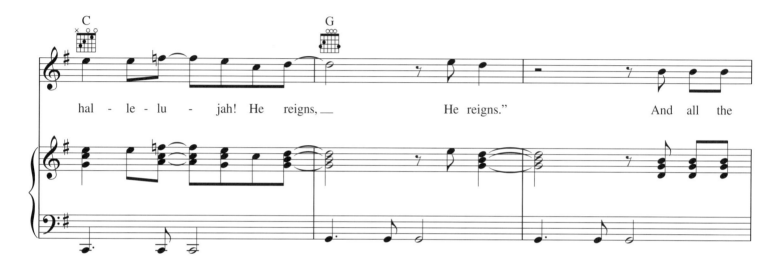

hal - le - lu - jah! He reigns, ___ He reigns." And all the

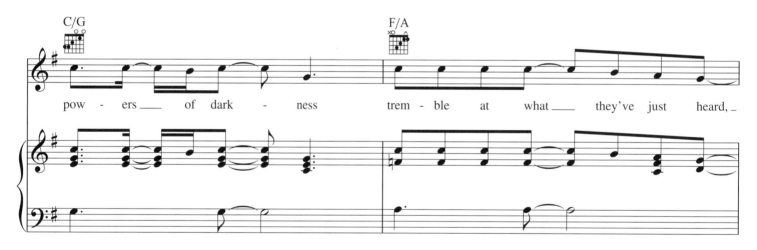

pow - ers ___ of dark - ness trem - ble at what ___ they've just heard, ___

___ 'cause all the

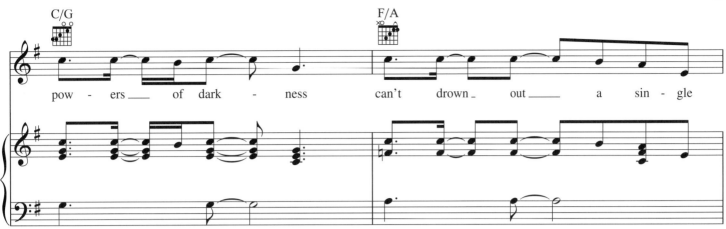

C/G   F/A

pow - ers __ of dark - ness can't drown _ out __ a sin - gle

G5

word. __   When all God's chil - dren sing out,

F   C   G

"Glo - ry, glo - ry, hal - le - lu - jah! He reigns, __ He reigns!"

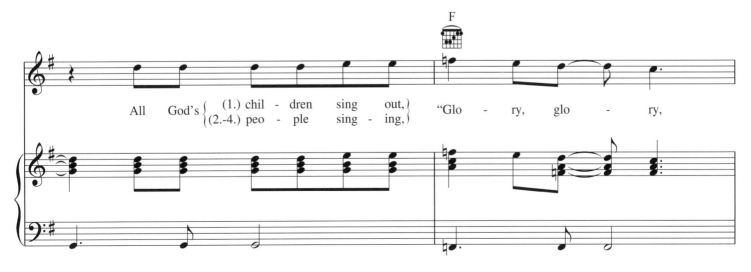

F

All God's { (1.) chil - dren sing out, } "Glo - ry, glo - ry,
        { (2.-4.) peo - ple sing - ing, }

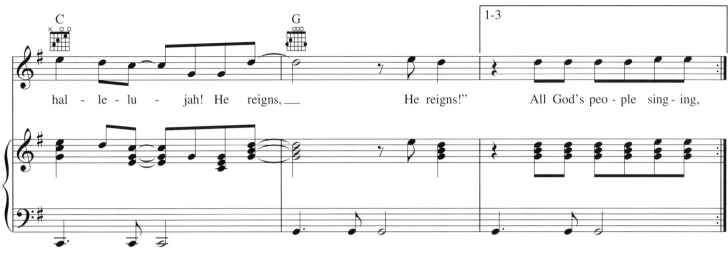

hal - le - lu - jah! He reigns, ___ He reigns!" All God's peo - ple sing - ing,

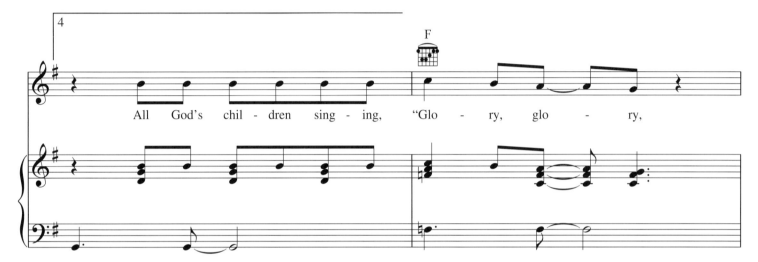

All God's chil - dren sing - ing, "Glo - ry, glo - ry,

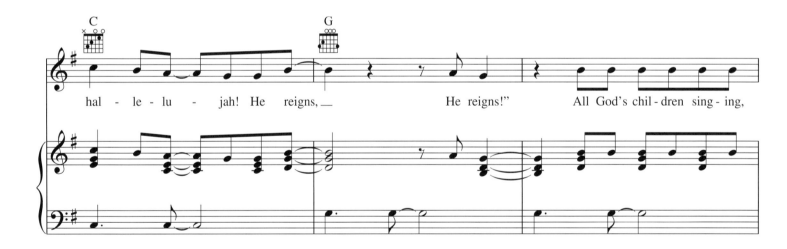

hal - le - lu - jah! He reigns, ___ He reigns!" All God's chil - dren sing - ing,

"Glo - ry, glo - ry, hal - le - lu - jah! He reigns!" ___

WHEREVER WE GO

Words and Music by TED TJORNHOM,
PHIL "JOEL" URRY, STEVE TAYLOR,
PETER FURLER and LYNN NICHOLS

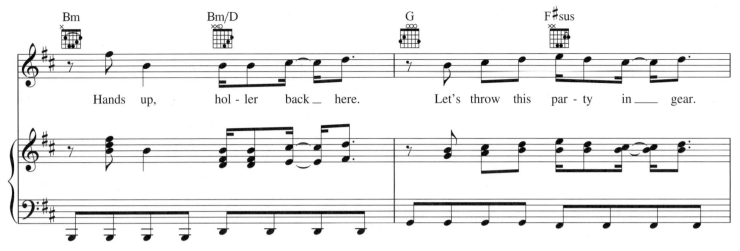

Hands up, hol-ler back __ here. Let's throw this par-ty in __ gear.

We brought the wel - come mat. Wher-ev-er we go, that's _ where the par-ty's at.

Hands up, hol-ler back __ now. We don't claim an-y know - how;

we've giv-en God __ all that. Wher-ev-er we go, that's _ where the par-ty's at.

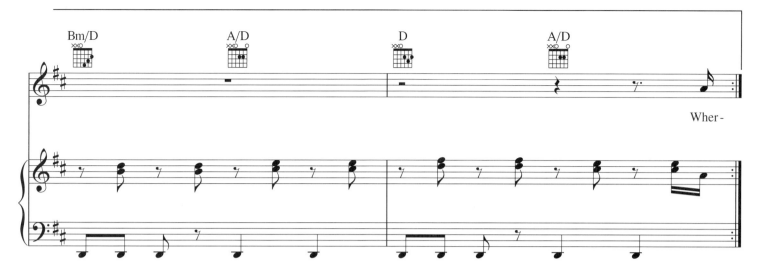

Wher-

ev - er we go, that's __ where the par - ty's at.

High, throw your hands up, throw your hands up high.

High, throw your hands up, throw your hands up high.

This is the mes-sage we spread, bring-ing life to the dead.

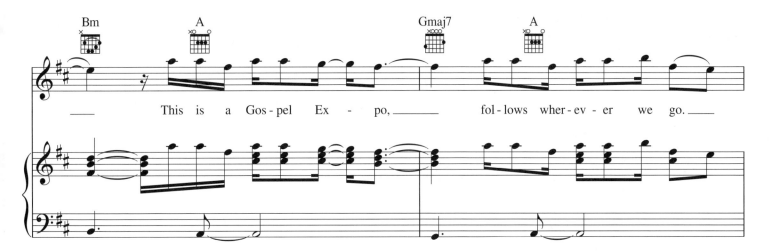

This is a Gos-pel Ex - po, fol-lows wher-ev-er we go.

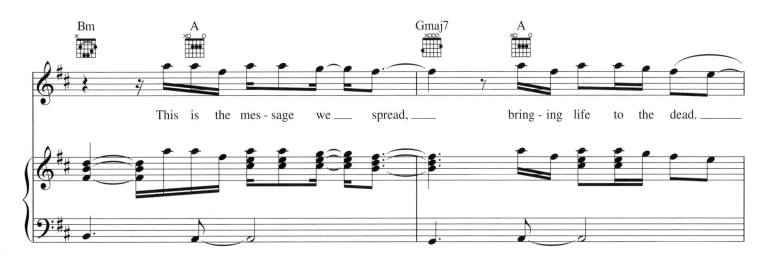

This is the mes-sage we spread, bring-ing life to the dead.

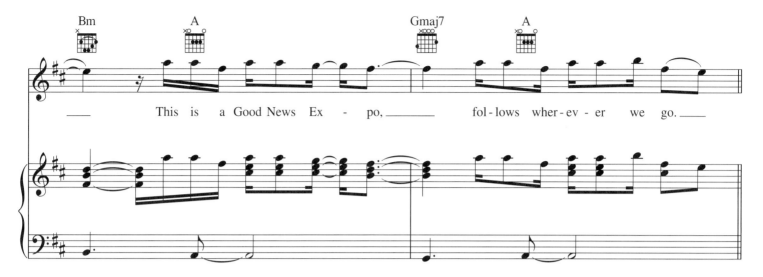

This is a Good News Ex - po, _____ fol - lows wher - ev - er we go. _____

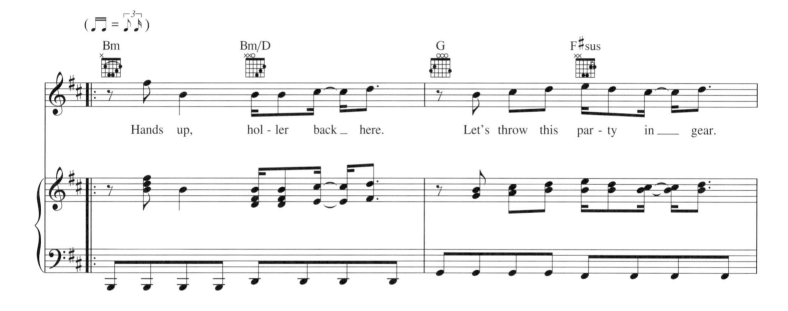

Hands up, hol - ler back _ here. Let's throw this par - ty in ___ gear.

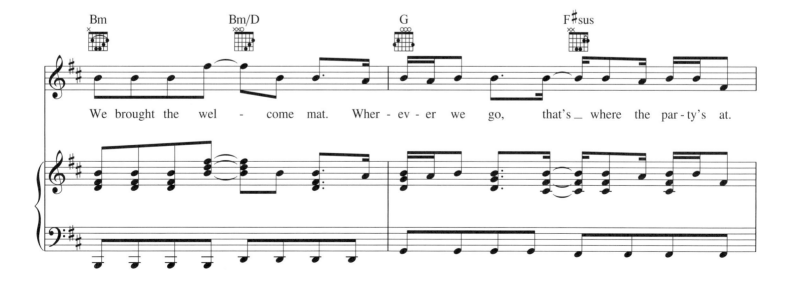

We brought the wel - come mat. Wher - ev - er we go, that's _ where the par - ty's at.

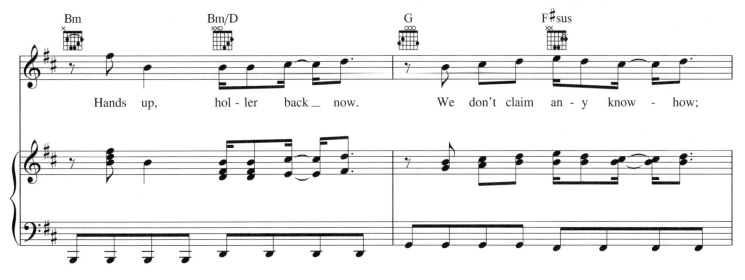

Hands up, hol - ler back __ now. We don't claim an - y know - how;

we've giv - en God __ all that. Wher - ev - er we go, that's __ where the par - ty's at.

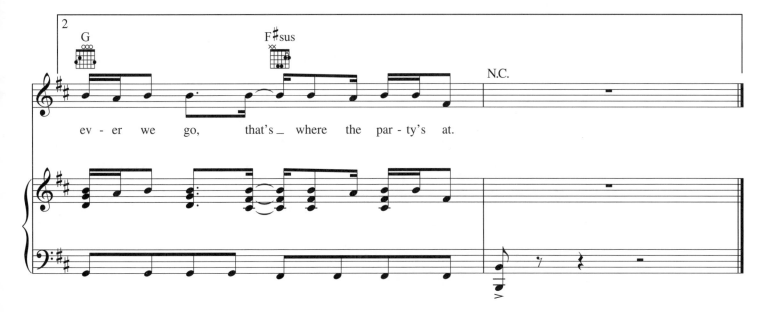

ev - er we go, that's __ where the par - ty's at.

TAKE ME TO YOUR LEADER

Words and Music by PETER FURLER
and STEVE TAYLOR

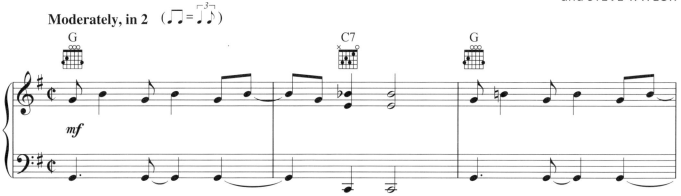

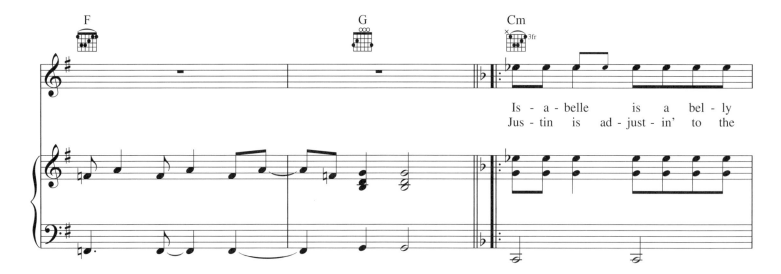

Is - a - belle   is   a   bel - ly
Jus - tin   is   ad - just - in' to the

dancer with a klep - to - ma - ni - ac's re - straint, tried steal - ing
o - dor from __ The - o - dore's Ev - er - green In - cense, but a - ro - ma -

Hel - e - na's hand bas - ket, made a fast get - a - way, but Mc-Queen she ain't. __
ther - a - py don't make him an - y young - er than __ Ol - i - ver's __ All Liv - er Sup - ple - ments. __

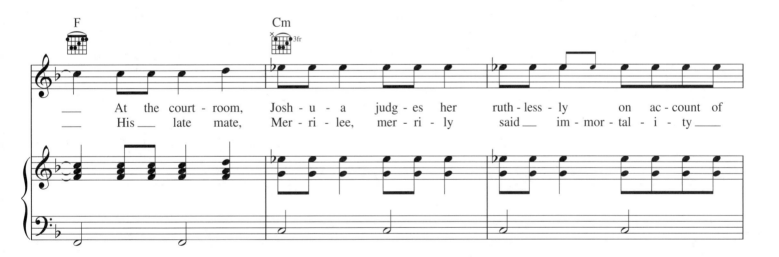

__ At the court - room, Josh - u - a judg - es her ruth - less - ly on ac - count of
__ His late mate, Mer - ri - lee, mer - ri - ly said __ im - mor - tal - i - ty __

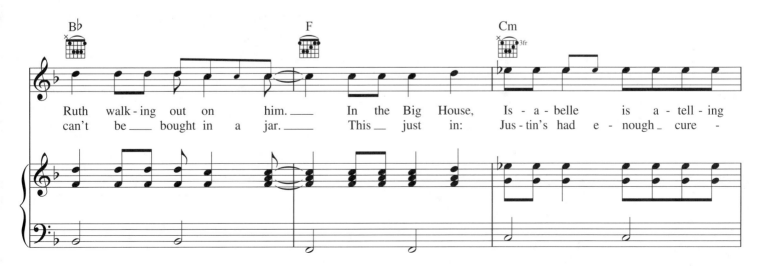

Ruth walk - ing out on him. __ In the Big House, Is - a - belle is a - tell - ing
can't be __ bought in a jar. __ This __ just in: Jus - tin's had e - nough __ cure -

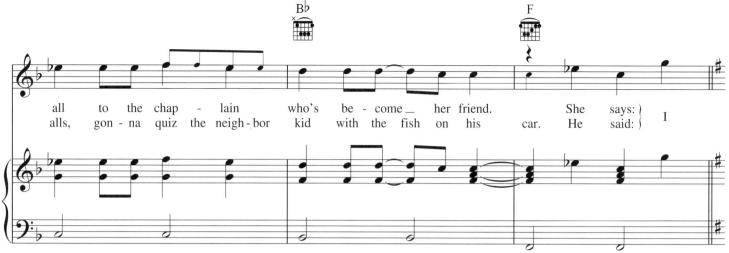

all to the chap - lain who's be - come __ her friend. She says: } I
alls, gon - na quiz the neigh - bor kid with the fish on his car. He said: }

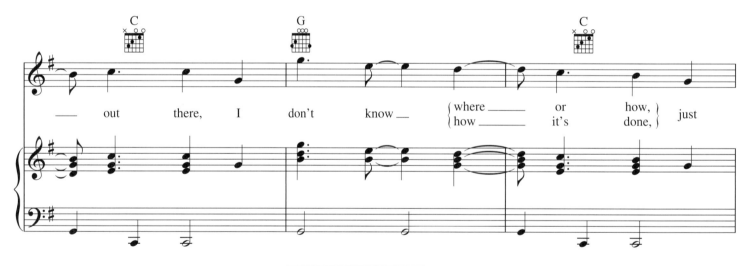

don't know __ why _____ you care, I don't know __ what's __

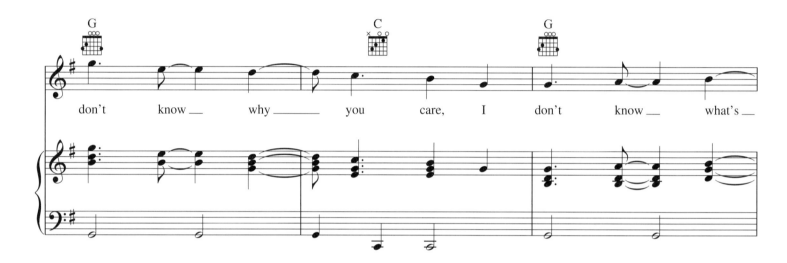

__ out there, I don't know __ { where _____ or how, } just
{ how _____ it's done, }

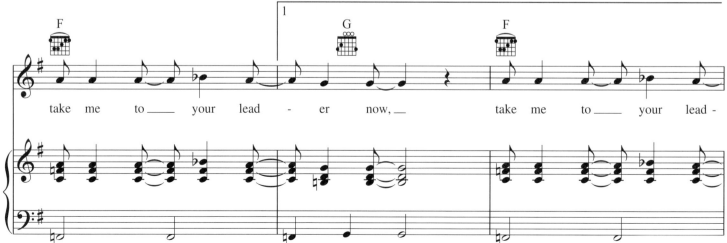

take me to ___ your lead - er now, ___ take me to ___ your lead -

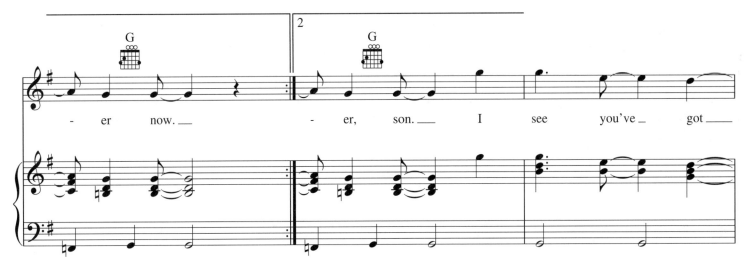

-er now. ___ -er, son. ___ I see you've ___ got ___

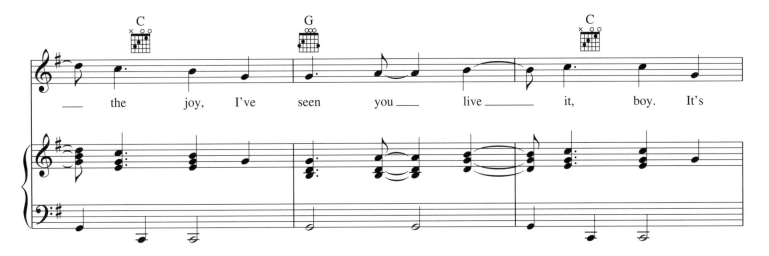

___ the joy, I've seen you ___ live ___ it, boy. It's

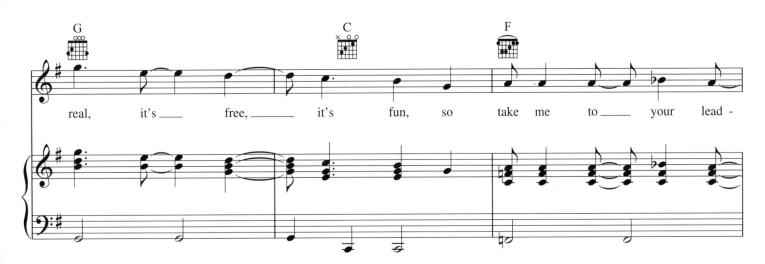

real, it's ___ free, _____ it's fun, so take me to ___ your lead -

-er, son. ___ Take me to ___ your lead - er, son. ___

They

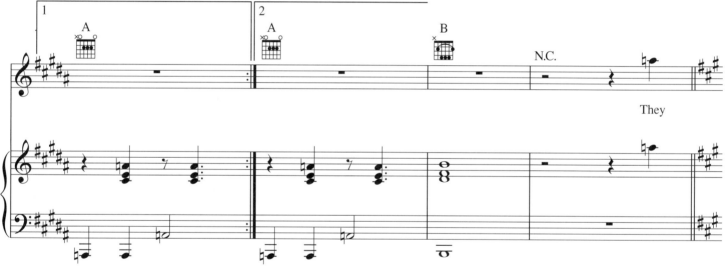

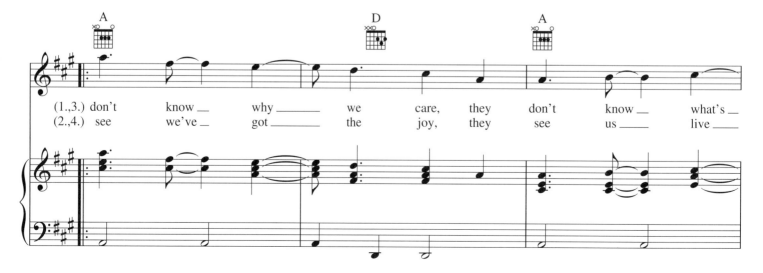

(1.,3.) don't know __ why __ we care, they don't know __ what's __

(2.,4.) see we've __ got __ the joy, they see us __ live __

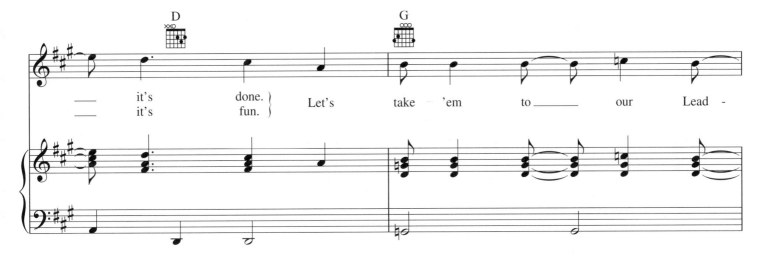

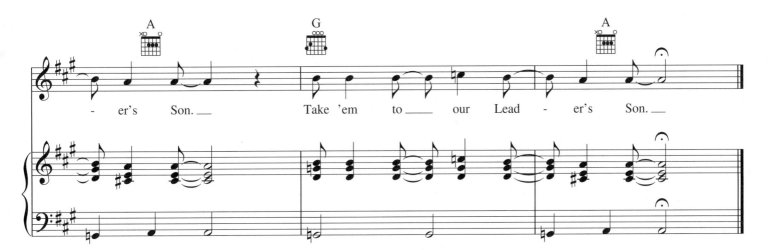

STAY STRONG

Words and Music by STEVE TAYLOR,
PETER FURLER and JEFF FRANKENSTEIN

Play cues 2nd time

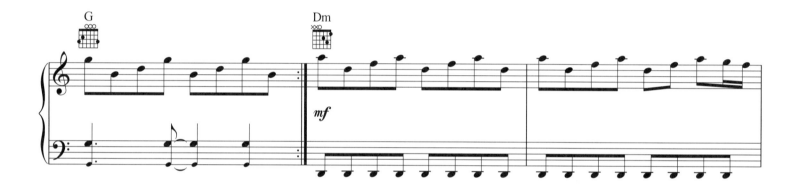

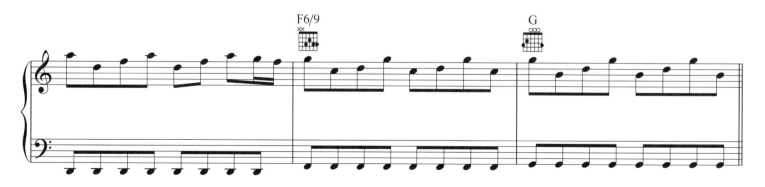

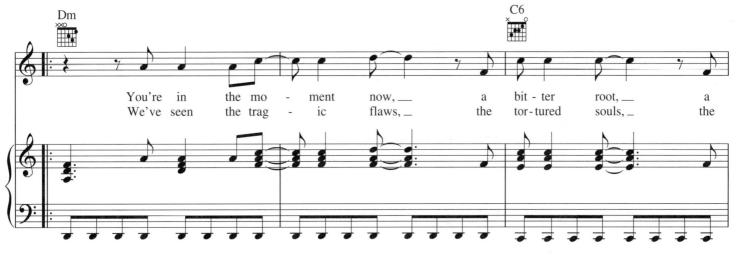

You're in the mo - ment now, __ a bit - ter root, __ a
We've seen the trag - ic flaws, __ the tor - tured souls, __ the

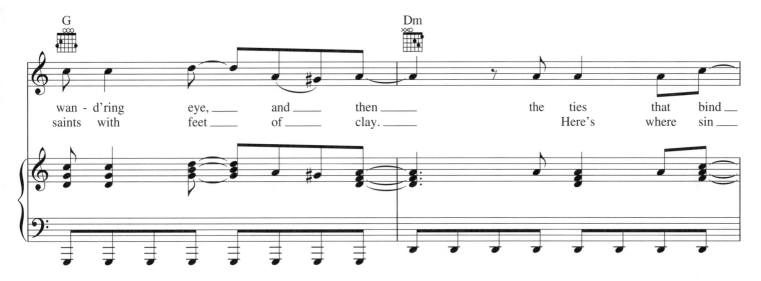

wan - d'ring eye, __ and __ then __ the ties that bind __
saints with feet __ of __ clay. __ Here's where sin __

__ start wear - ing __ thin __ with - in. __
__ be - comes __ cli - ché. __ We've

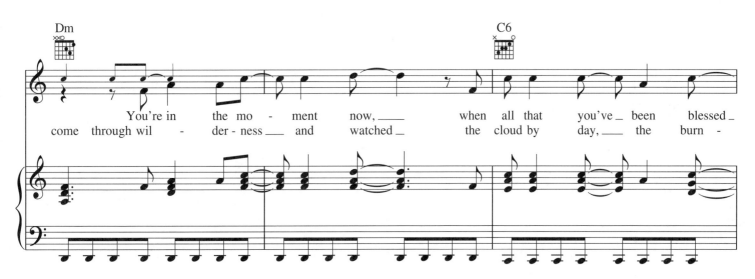

You're in the mo - ment now, __ when all that you've __ been blessed __
come through wil - der - ness __ and watched __ the cloud by day, __ the burn -

with is _____ not e - nough. _____ Here's where the ground ___
- ing sky _____ in - to dawn. _____ Have you for - got -

___ gets loose, ___ here's where the dev - ils call ___ your bluff.
- ten who ___ you are? Did you for - get ___ whose trip ___ you're on?

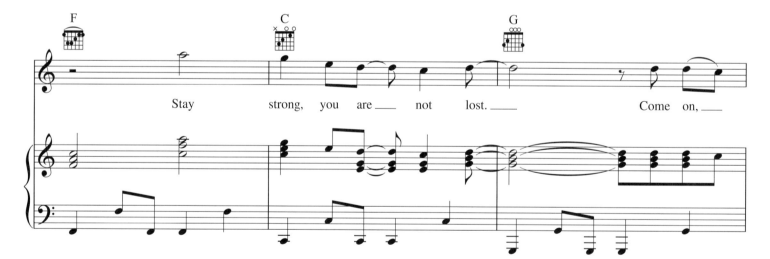

Stay strong, you are ___ not lost. _____ Come on, ___

fix your __ eyes __ a - head. There's a ____ new dawn ___ to light __ our day, ___

our day. ___ We've got-ta ___ stay

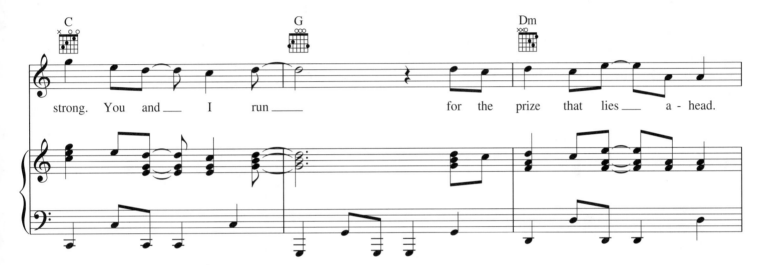

strong. You and ___ I run ___ for the prize that lies ___ a-head.

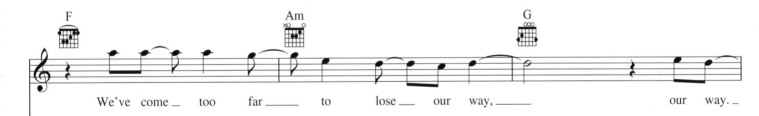

We've come ___ too far ___ to lose ___ our way, ___ our way. ___

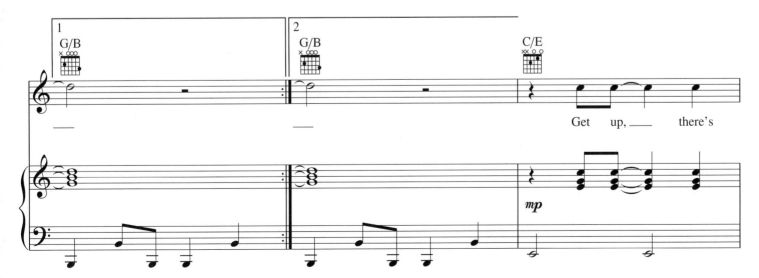

Get up, ___ there's

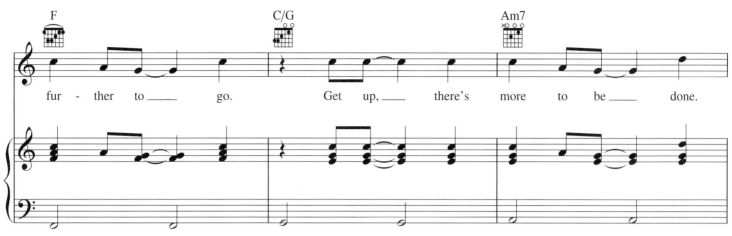

fur - ther to ____ go. Get up, ____ there's more to be ____ done.

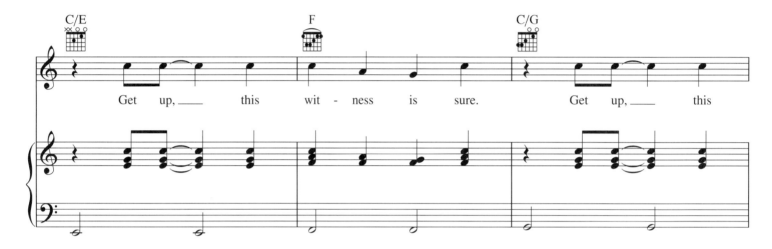

Get up, ____ this wit - ness is sure. Get up, ____ this

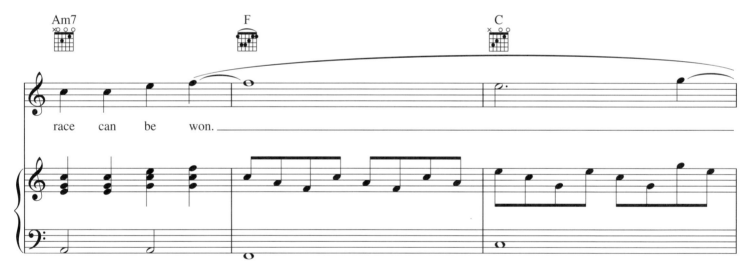

race can be won. ____

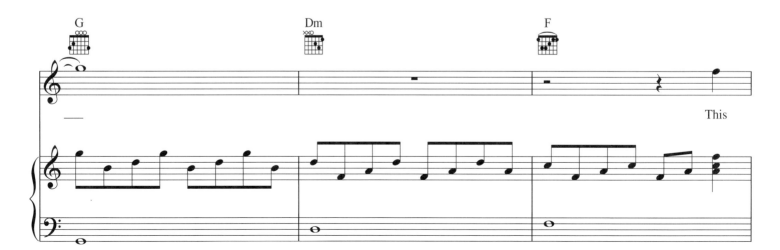

This

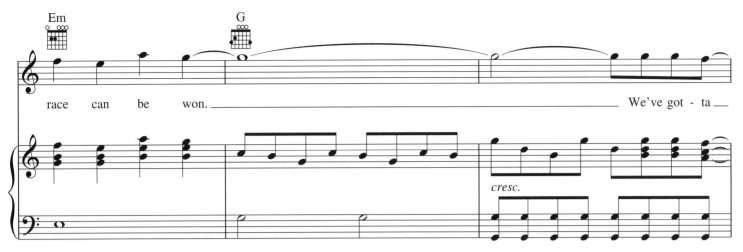

race can be won. _____ We've got - ta ___

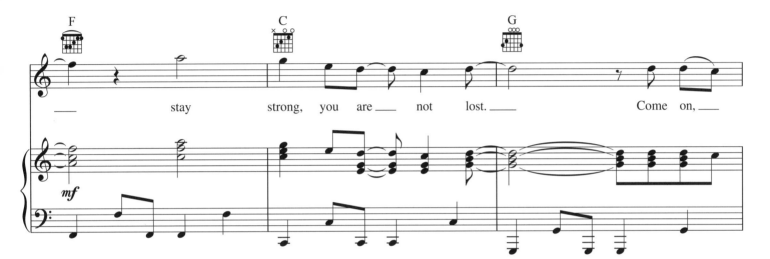

___ stay strong, you are ___ not lost. ___ Come on, ___

fix your ___ eyes ___ a - head. Our Fa - ther's dawn ___ will light ___ our day, ___

___ our day. ___ Come on, and ___ stay

strong. His grip ___ is sure, ___ and His pa - tience still ___ en - dures.

There'll be ___ no let - ting go ___ to - day, _____ no way. __

___ Oh, ___ come on and ___ stay strong. You and ___ I run __

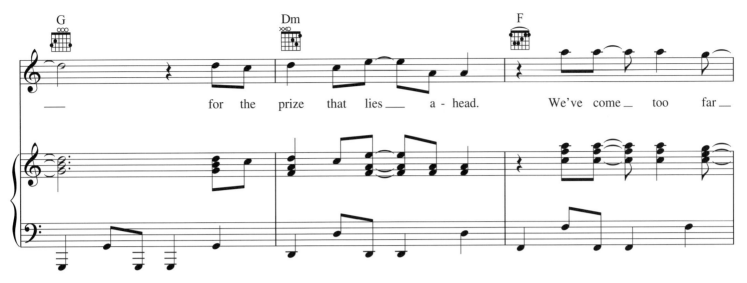

for the prize that lies ___ a - head. We've come ___ too far ___

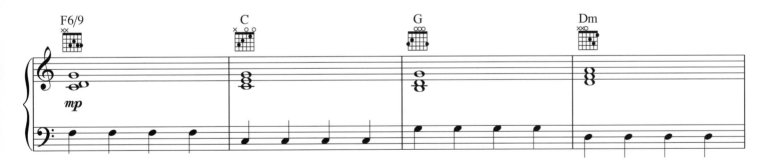

___ to lose ___ our way, _____ our way. ___

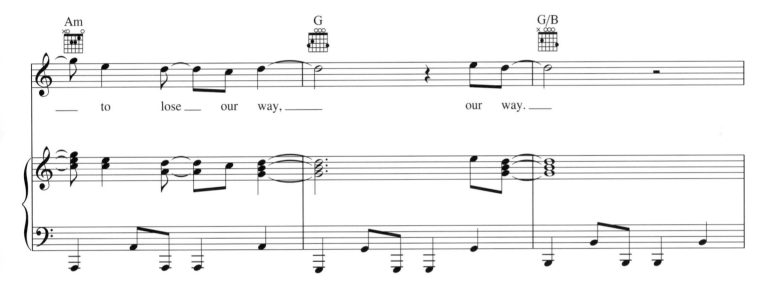

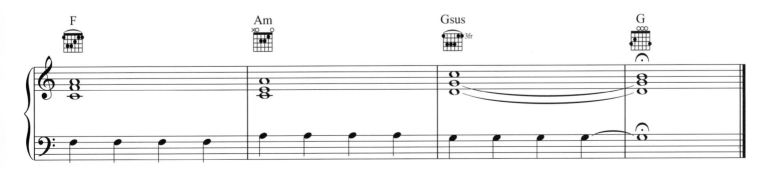

YOU ARE MY KING
(Amazing Love)

Words and Music by
BILLY JAMES FOOTE

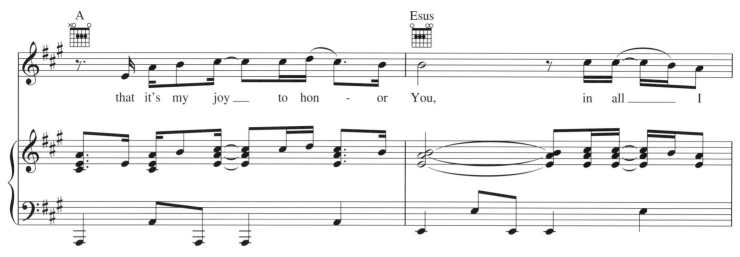

that it's my joy ___ to hon - or You, in all ___ I

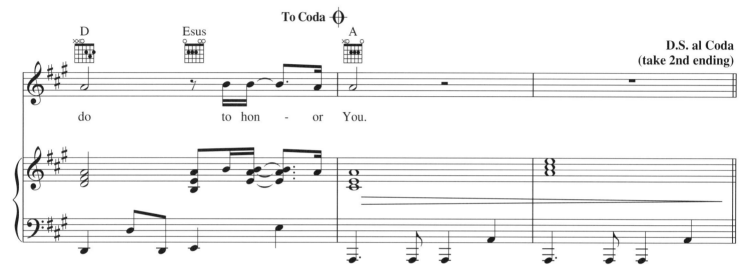

do to hon - or You.

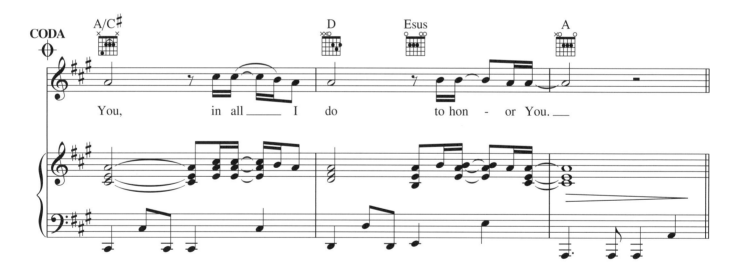

You, in all ___ I do to hon - or You. ___

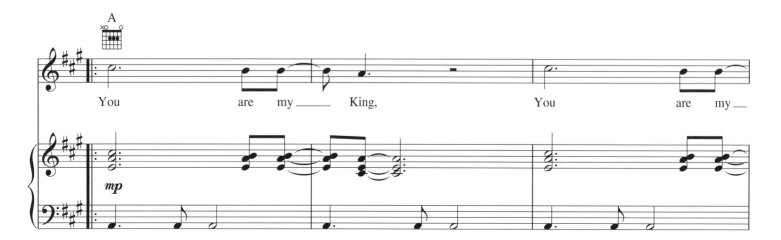

You are my ___ King, You are my ___

King. Je - sus, ___ King. (A - maz - ing love.) ___ A - maz-ing love, ___ how ___

___ can it be _____ that You, my King, ___ should die ___ for me? ___

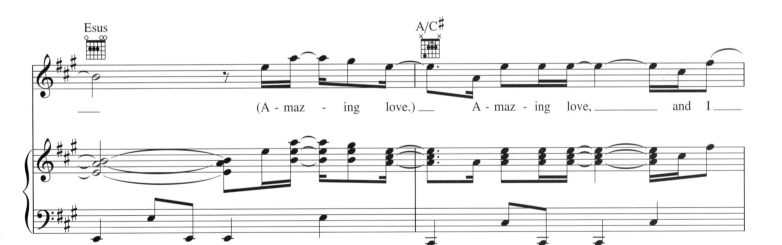

___ (A - maz - ing love.) ___ A - maz - ing love, _____ and I ___

___ know it's true, _____ that it's my joy ___ to hon - or You. ___

(A - maz - ing love.) _ _ In all _____ I do to hon - or

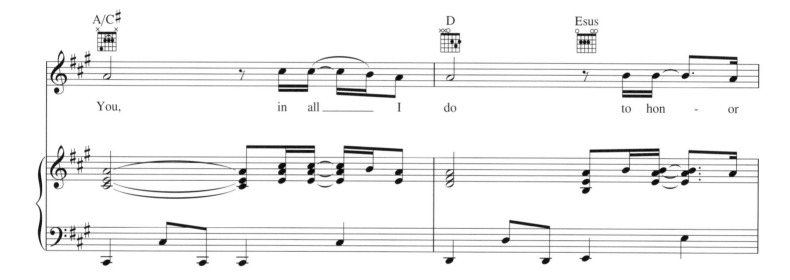

You, in all _____ I do to hon - or

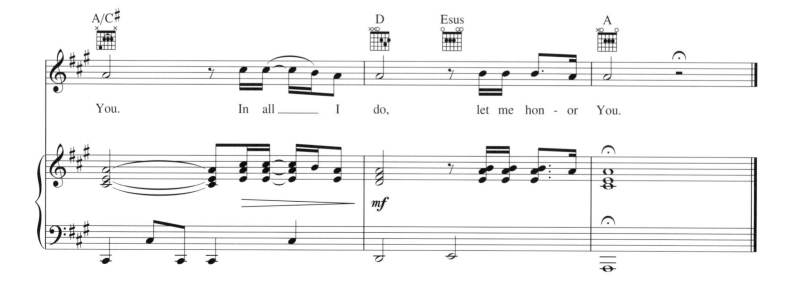

You. In all _____ I do, let me hon - or You.

ENTERTAINING ANGELS

Words and Music by PETER FURLER,
PHIL URRY and JODY DAVIS

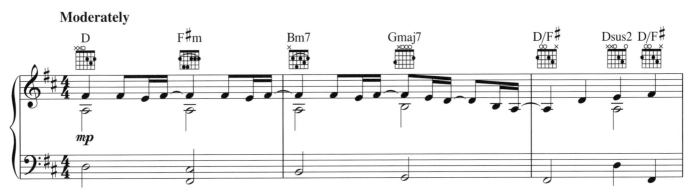

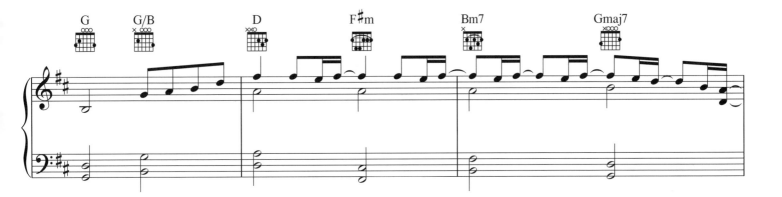

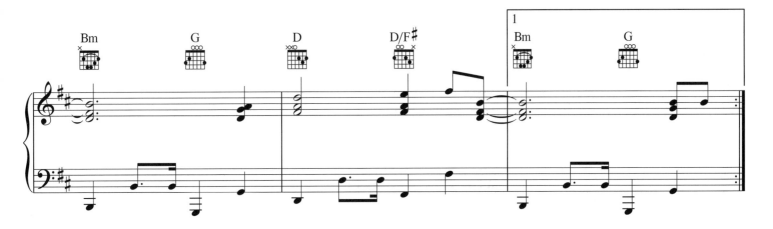

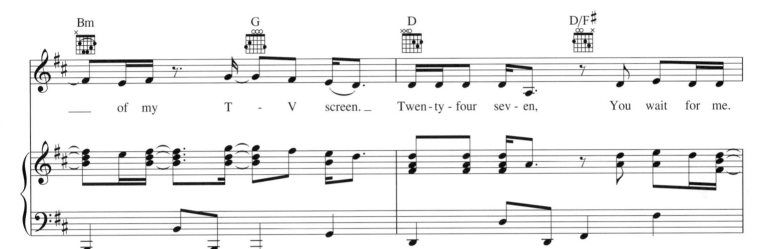

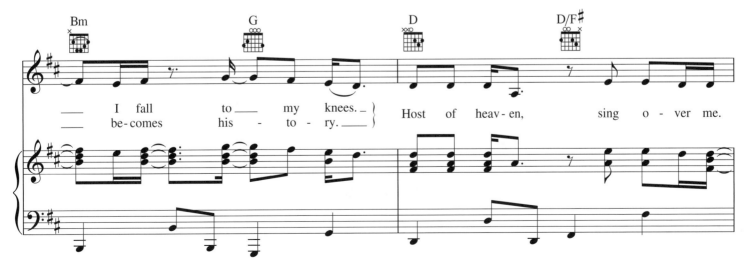

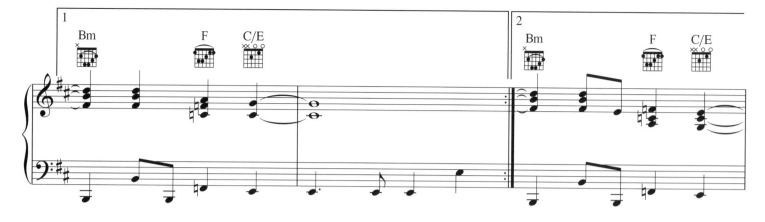

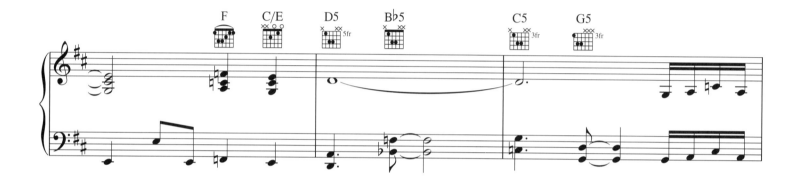

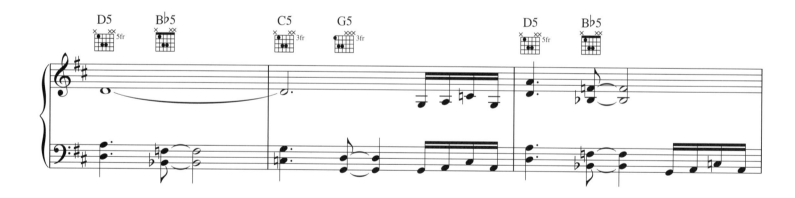

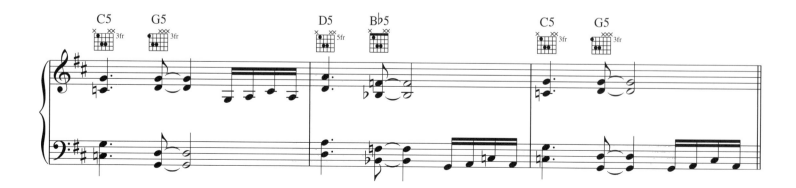

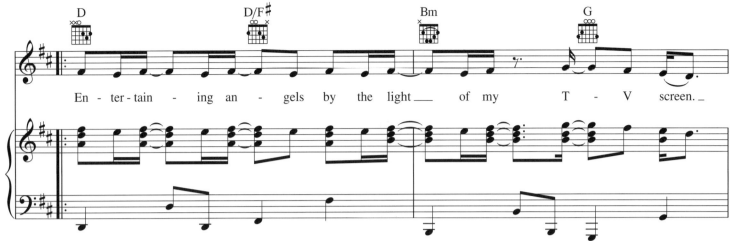

En - ter - tain - ing an - gels by the light ___ of my T - V screen. ___

Twen - ty - four sev - en, You wait for me.

En - ter - tain - ing an - gels {by the time ___ I fall to ___ my knees. ___}
{while the night ___ be - comes his - to - ry. ___}

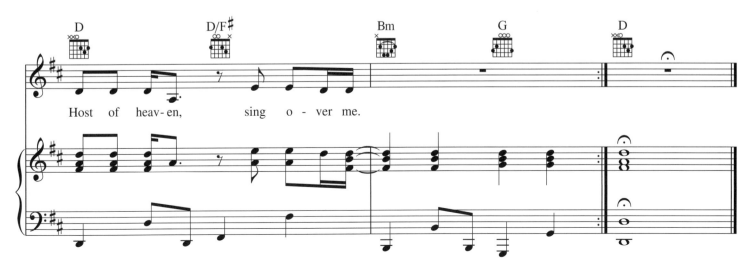

Host of heav - en, sing o - ver me.

REALITY

Words and Music by PETER FURLER
and STEVE TAYLOR

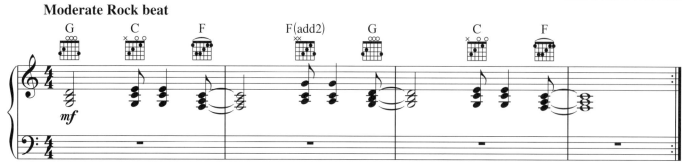

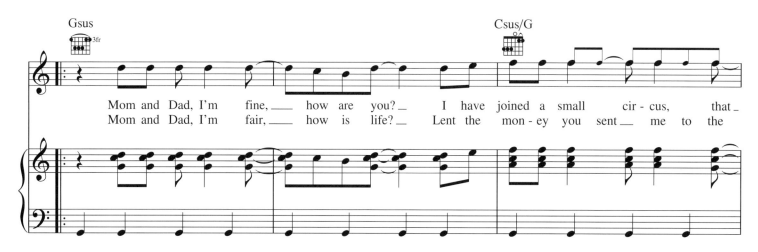

Mom and Dad, I'm fine, ___ how are you? ___ I have joined a small cir-cus, that ___
Mom and Dad, I'm fair, ___ how is life? ___ Lent the mon-ey you sent ___ me to the

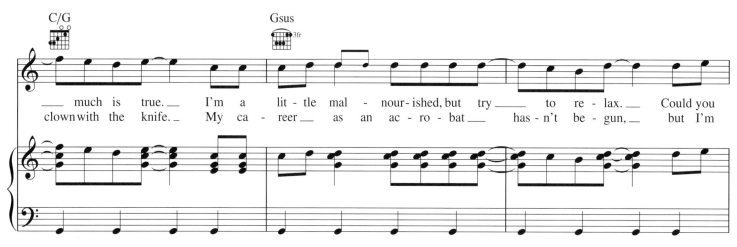

___ much is true. ___ I'm a lit-tle mal-nour-ished, but try ___ to re-lax. ___ Could you
clown with the knife. My ca-reer ___ as an ac-ro-bat ___ has-n't be-gun, ___ but I'm

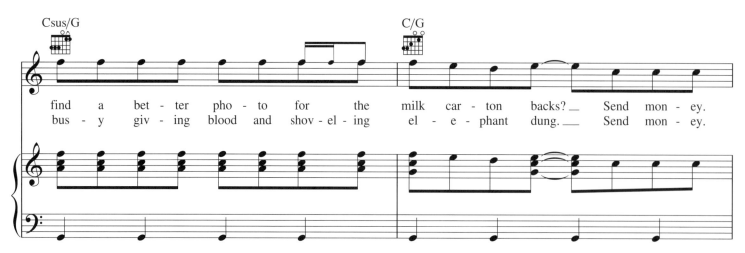

find a bet-ter pho-to for the milk car-ton backs? ___ Send mon-ey.
bus-y giv-ing blood and shov-el-ing el-e-phant dung. ___ Send mon-ey.

Run - a - way, where's __ your head? Dream - ers' dreams
Run - a - way, why ____ so tense? Dream - ers' dreams

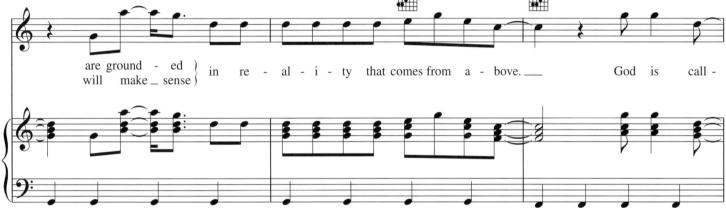

are ground - ed } in re - al - i - ty that comes from a - bove. ___ God is call -
will make __ sense }

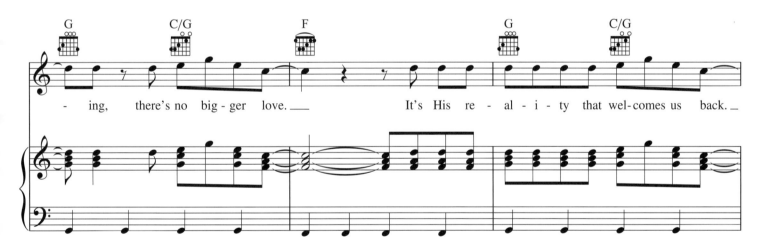

- ing, there's no big - ger love. ___ It's His re - al - i - ty that wel - comes us back. __

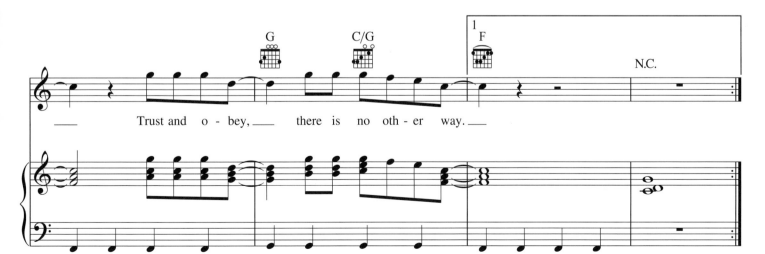

Trust and o - bey, ___ there is no oth - er way. ___

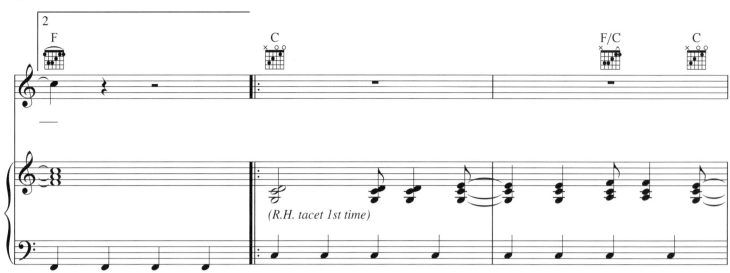

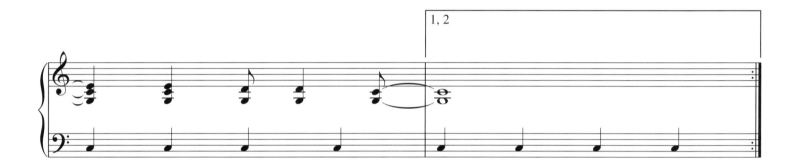

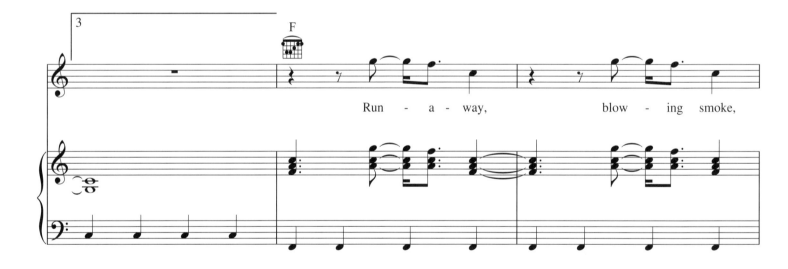

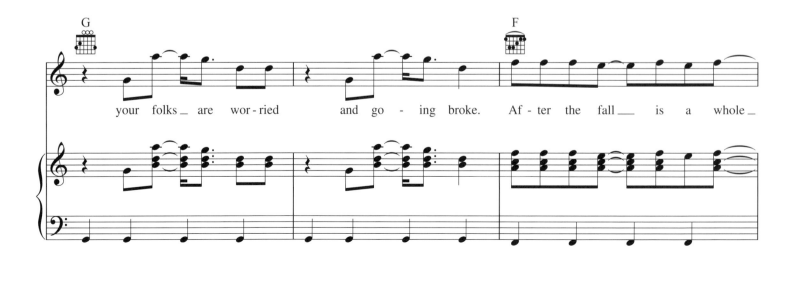

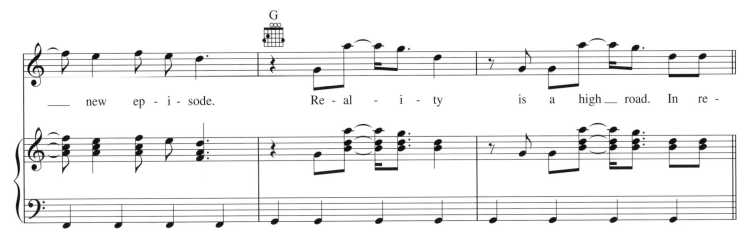

new ep - i - sode. Re - al - i - ty is a high road. In re -

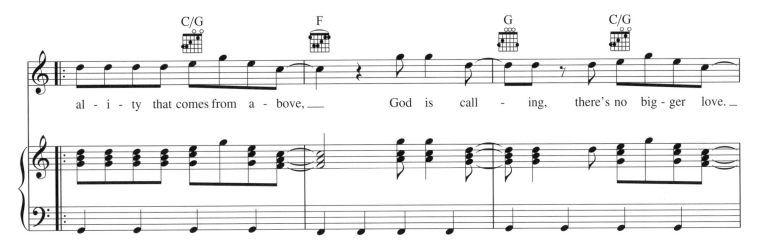

al - i - ty that comes from a - bove, ___ God is call - ing, there's no big - ger love. ___

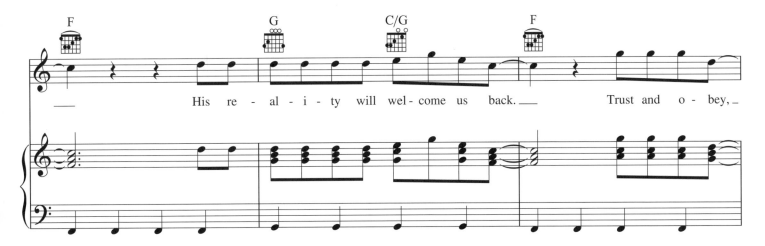

His re - al - i - ty will wel - come us back. ___ Trust and o - bey, ___

Repeat and Fade **Optional Ending**

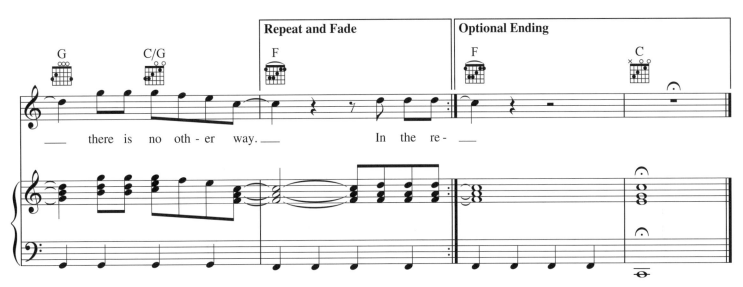

___ there is no oth - er way. ___ In the re - ___

REAL GOOD THING

Words and Music by PETER FURLER,
STEVE TAYLOR and JODY DAVIS

Born to ___ sin ___ and ___ then get ___ caught. ___ All our ___ good ___ deeds
Doc - tor's ___ com - ing, ___ look - ing ___ grim. ___ "Do you ___ have ___ a

don't mean ___ squat. ___ Sell the Vol - vo, shred the Vi - sa,
fa - v'rite ___ hymn?" ___ Check your bal - ance through the years, ___

send the cash ___ to Ma Te - re - sa. Great i - dea; ___ the on - ly catch ___ is, you
all ac - counts ___ are in ar - rears. ___ Guilt is bit - ter, grace is sweet. ___

don't get saved on mer - it badg - es. ___ When we

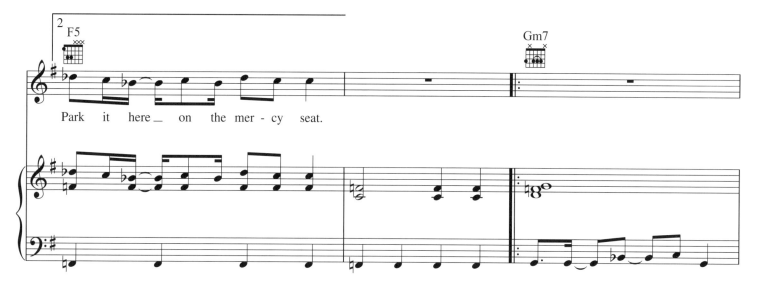

Park it here on the mer-cy seat.

When we don't get what we de - serve,

that's a real good thing, ___ a real good thing. When we

get what ___ we don't de - serve, ___ that's a real good thing, ___ a real good

1, 2 thing.

3 When we thing.

JOY

Words and Music by PETER FURLER
and STEVE TAYLOR

Moderately fast

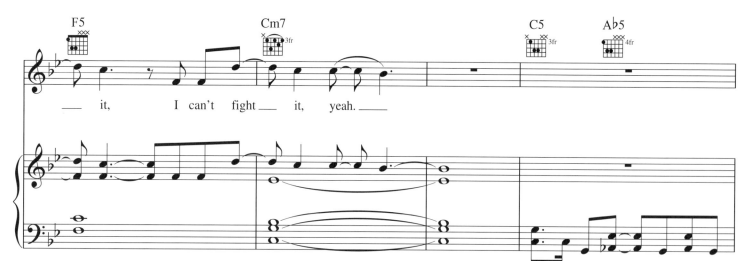

Recorded a half step higher.

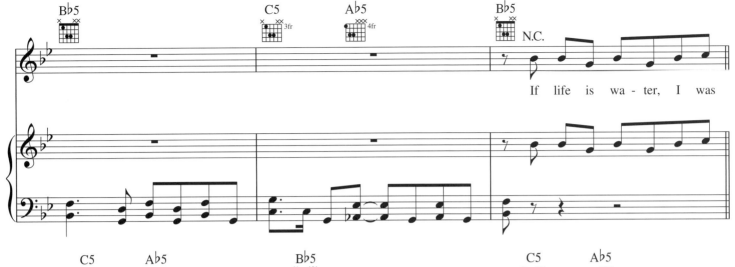

If life is wa - ter, I was

dry as Tuc - son dirt. If it's a gam - ble, I'd al - read - y lost___ my shirt.
va - sion is___ com - plete. If it's a rhy - thm, I have found the per - fect beat.

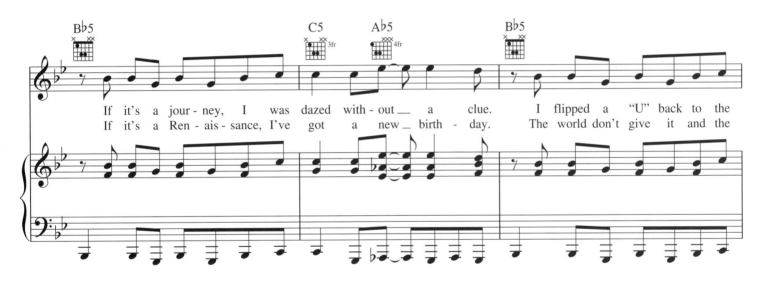

If it's a jour - ney, I was dazed with - out___ a clue. I flipped a "U" back to the
If it's a Ren - ais - sance, I've got a new___ birth - day. The world don't give it and the

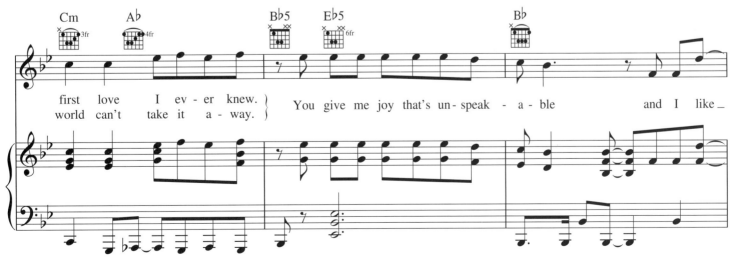

first love I ev - er knew. } You give me joy that's un - speak - a - ble and I like___
world can't take it a - way. }

it, and I like ___ it, yeah. ___ Your love for me's ir - re - sist -

i - ble; I can't fight ___ it, I can't fight ___ it, yeah. ___

You car - ried the cross and took my shame; I be - lieve ___ it, I be - lieve ___

___ it, yeah. ___ You shine Your light of a - maz - ing grace; I re - ceive ___

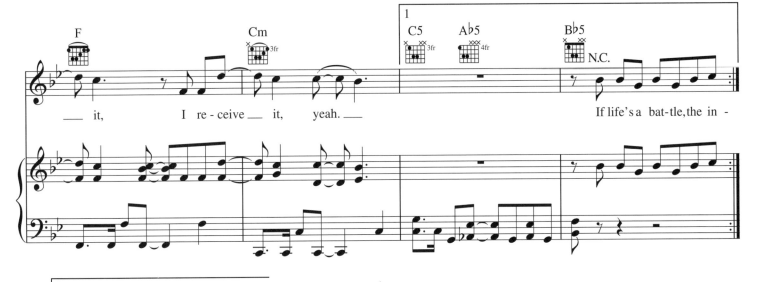

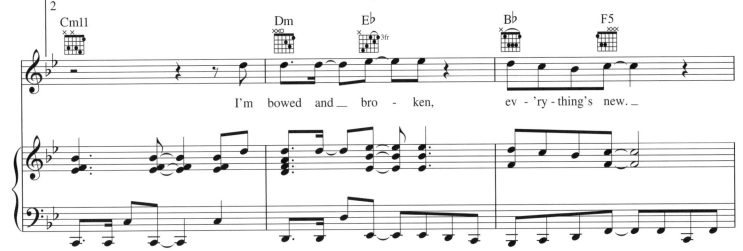

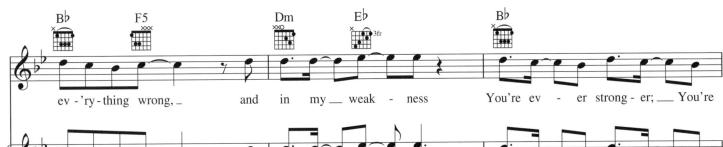

pull - ing __ me back where __ I _____ be - long. _____

You give me joy that's un - speak - a - ble, and I like ___ it, and I like ___ it, yeah. ___

Your love for me's ir - re - sist - i - ble; I can't fight ___ it, I can't fight __

__ it. You car - ried the cross and took my shame; I be - lieve __

it, I be - lieve ___ it, yeah. ___ You shine Your light of a - maz -

ing grace; I re - ceive ___ it, I re - ceive ___ it, yeah. ___

You give me joy that's un - speak - a - ble, and I like ___ it, and I like ___

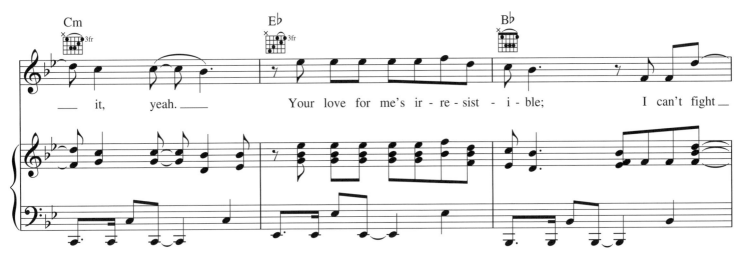

it, yeah. ___ Your love for me's ir - re - sist - i - ble; I can't fight ___

it, I can't fight __ it, yeah. __ You car - ried the cross and took

my shame; I be - lieve __ it, I be - lieve __ it, yeah. __

You shine Your light of a - maz - ing grace; I re - ceive __ it, I re - ceive __

Optional Ending

Repeat ad lib. and Fade

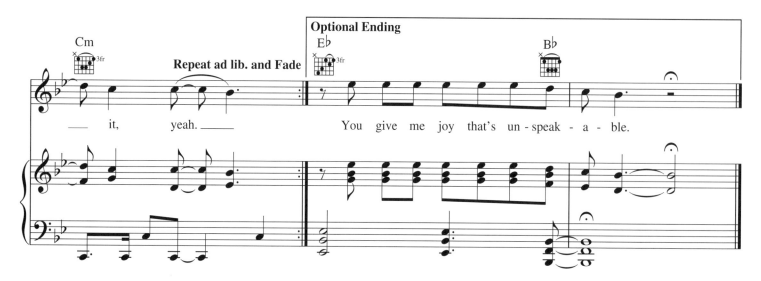

__ it, yeah. __ You give me joy that's un - speak - a - ble.

IT IS YOU

Words and Music by
PETER FURLER

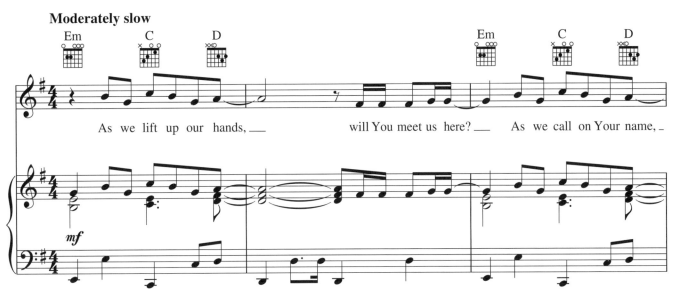

Moderately slow

As we lift up our hands, ___ will You meet us here? ___ As we call on Your name, ___

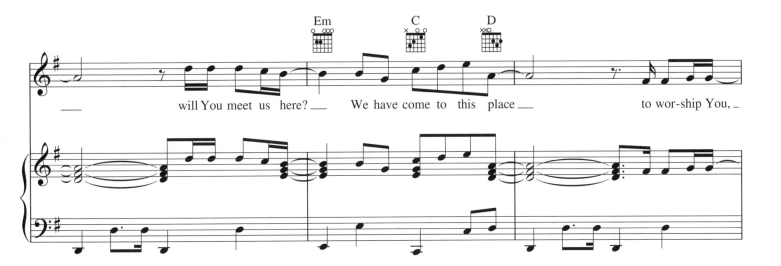

will You meet us here? ___ We have come to this place ___ to wor-ship You, ___

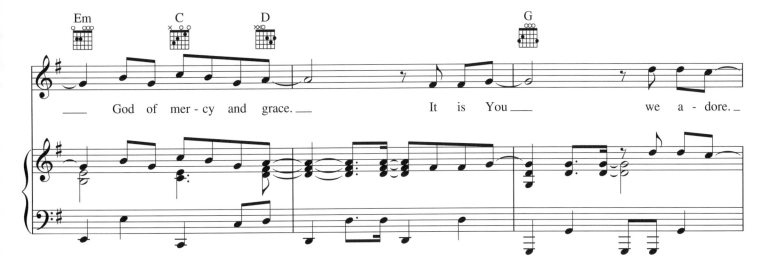

___ God of mer-cy and grace. ___ It is You ___ we a - dore. ___

It is You ___ prais - es are for, ___ on - ly You. ___

___ The heav - ens de - clare ___ it is You, ___ it is You. ___

___ And ho - ly, ho - ly is our God Al-might - y, ___

and ho - ly, ho - ly is His name a - lone, yeah, ___ And ho - ly, ho - ly is our

God Al-might - y, _____ and ho - ly, ho - ly is His name a - lone. It is You _

_____ we a - dore. _____ It is You, _____ on - ly You. _

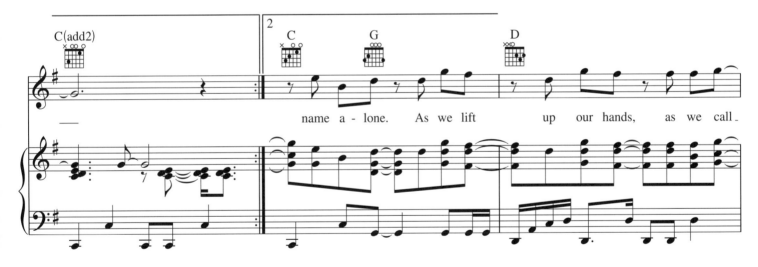

_____ name a - lone. As we lift up our hands, as we call _

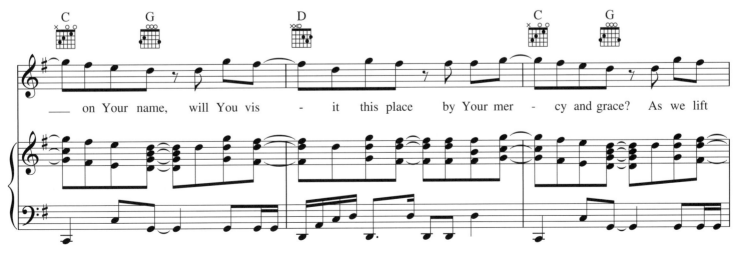

_____ on Your name, will You vis - it this place by Your mer - cy and grace? As we lift

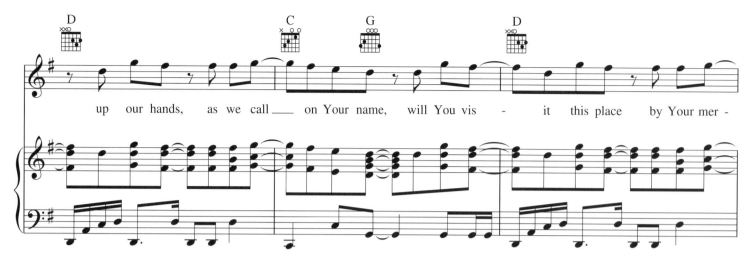

up our hands, as we call on Your name, will You vis - it this place by Your mer -

- cy and grace? It is You we a - dore. It is You.

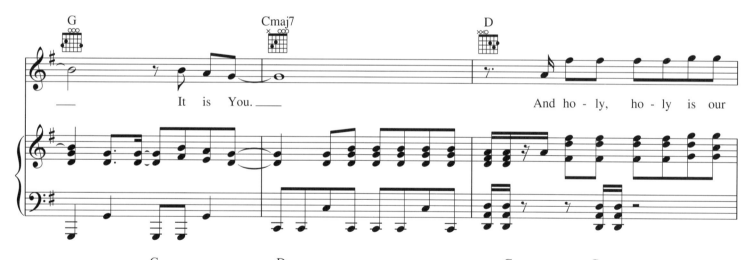

It is You. And ho - ly, ho - ly is our

God Al-might - y, and ho - ly, ho - ly is His name a - lone. (Ho - ly, ho - ly is our

SPIRIT THING

Words and Music by PETER FURLER
and STEVE TAYLOR

Upbeat Pop feel

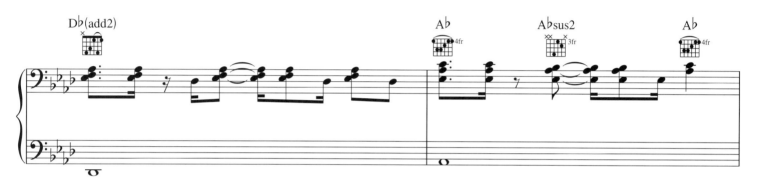

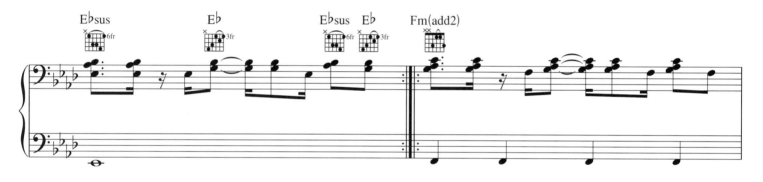

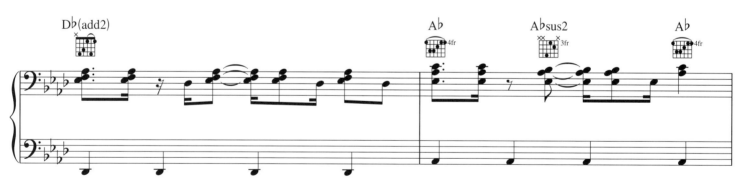

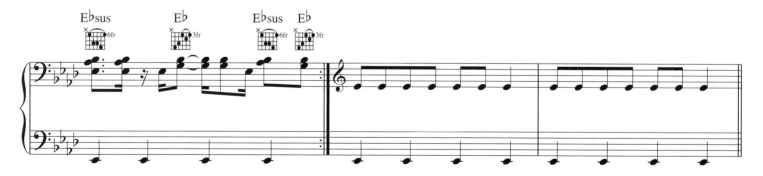

It's not a fam-'ly trait, ___ it's noth-ing that I ate, ___
It push-es when I quit, ___ it smells a coun-ter-feit. ___

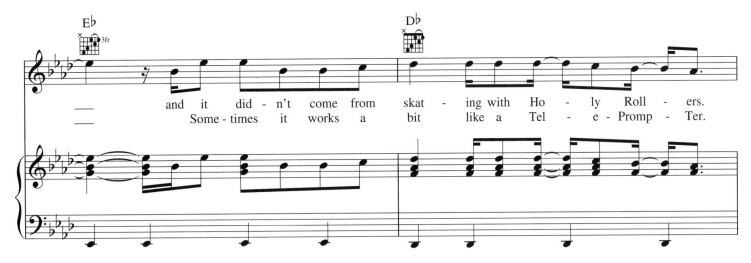

___ and it did-n't come from skat-ing with Ho-ly Roll-ers.
___ Some-times it works a bit like a Tel-e-Promp-Ter.

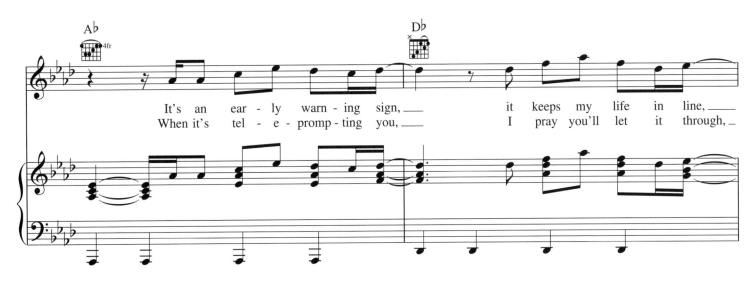

It's an ear-ly warn-ing sign, ___ it keeps my life in line, ___
When it's tel-e-promp-ting you, ___ I pray you'll let it through, ___

___ but it's so hard to de-fine. ___ Nev-er mind, ___ it's just a
___ and I'll help you with the how. ___ But for now, ___ it's just a

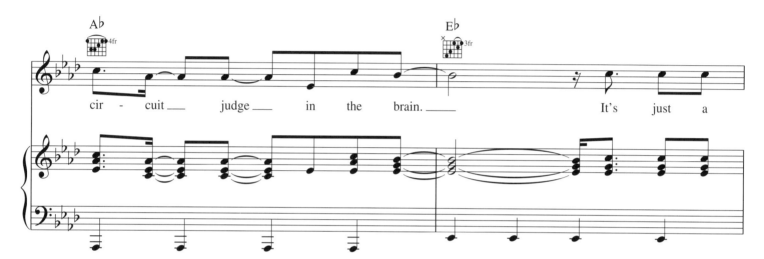

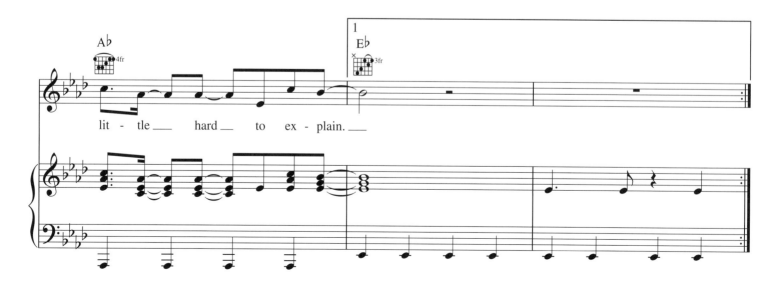

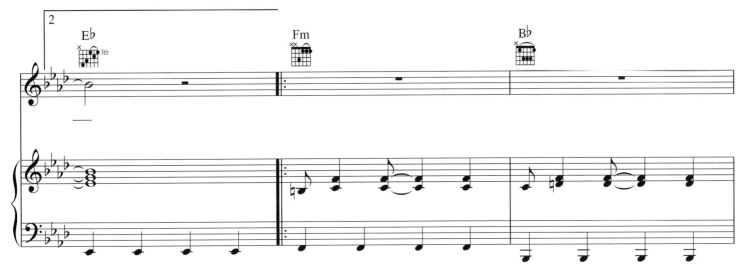

I took the pul -

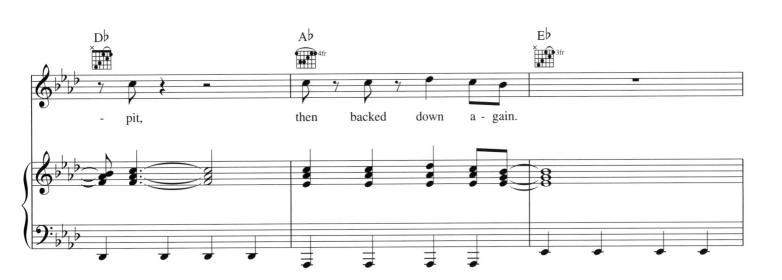

- pit, then backed down a - gain.

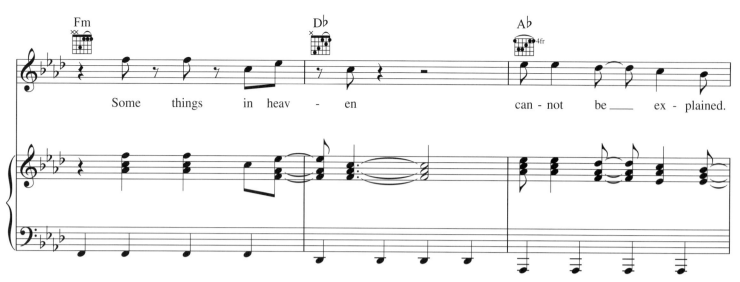

Some things in heav - en can - not be ___ ex - plained.

Yeah, ___ it's just a Spir - it ___ thing, ___ it's just a

ho - ly ___ nudge, it's like a cir - cuit ___ judge ___ in the brain. ___

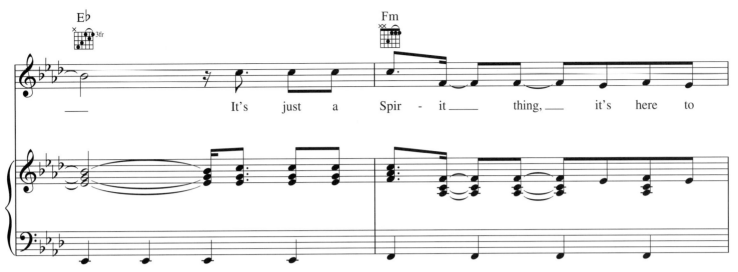

It's just a Spir - it ___ thing, ___ it's here to

guard my ___ heart, ___ it's just a lit - tle ___ hard ___ to ex - plain. ___

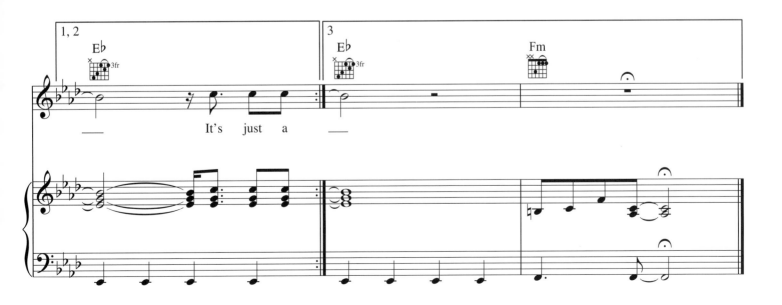

It's just a

I'M NOT ASHAMED

Words and Music by PETER FURLER
and STEVE TAYLOR

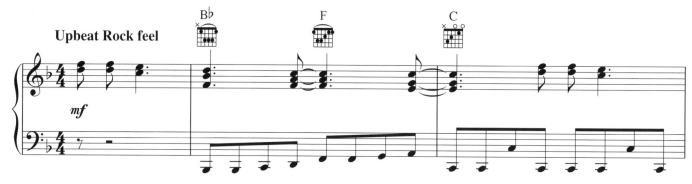

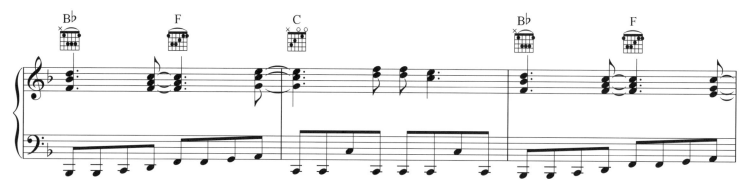

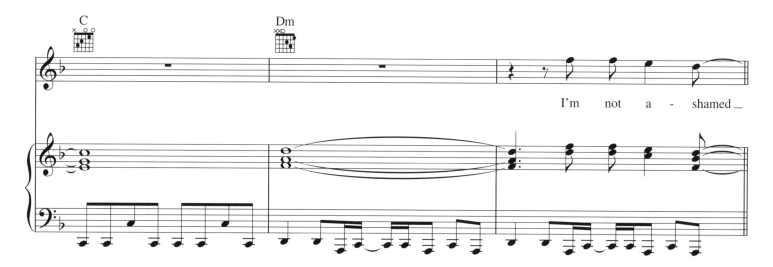

I'm not a - shamed __

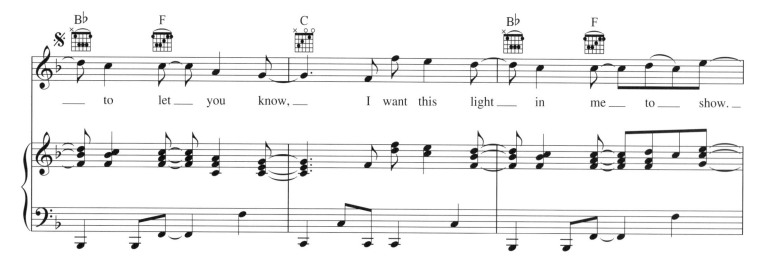

__ to let __ you know, __ I want this light __ in me __ to __ show. __

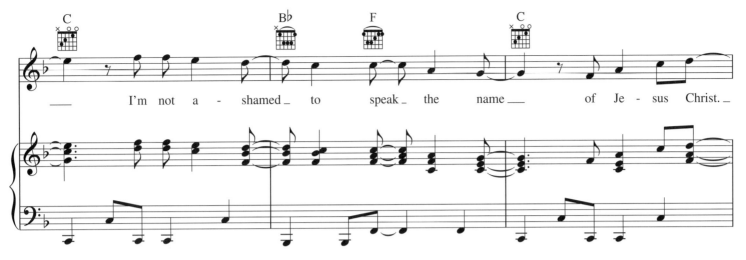

I'm not a - shamed _ to speak _ the name _ of Je - sus Christ. _

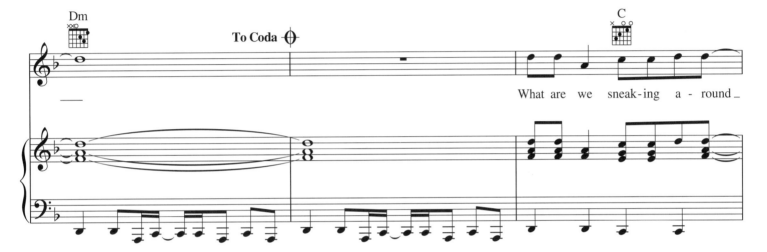

To Coda ⊕

What are we sneak-ing a - round _

_ for? Who are we try - ing to please, _

shrug-ging off sin, a - pol-o-giz - ing like we're spread-ing some kind of dis - ease?

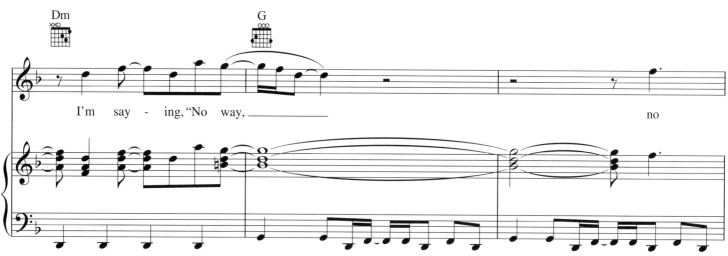

I'm say - ing, "No way, _____ no

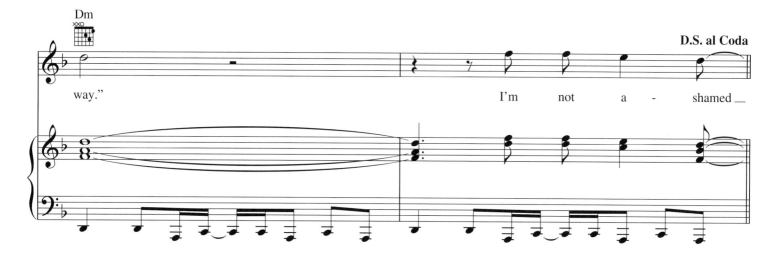

D.S. al Coda

way." I'm not a - shamed __

CODA

This one says, "It's a lost __ cause, save your

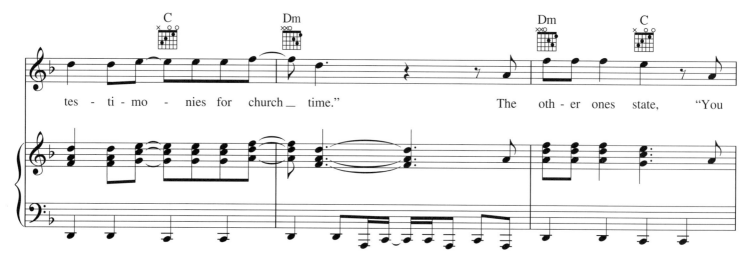

tes - ti - mo - nies for church __ time." The oth - er ones state, "You

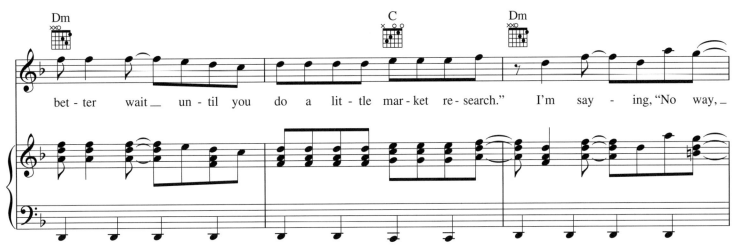

better wait_ un-til you do a lit-tle mar-ket re-search." I'm say - ing, "No way,_

no way."

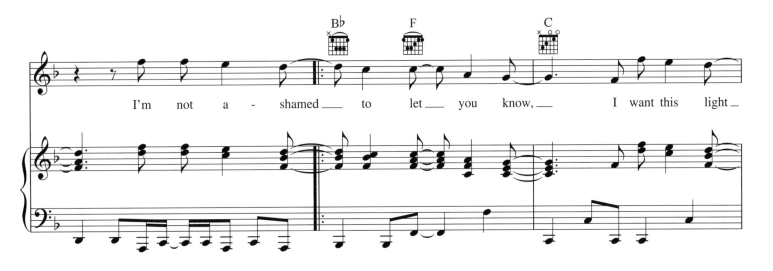

I'm not a-shamed _ to let_ you know, _ I want this light_

_ in me _ to _ show. _ I'm not a - shamed _ to speak_ the name_

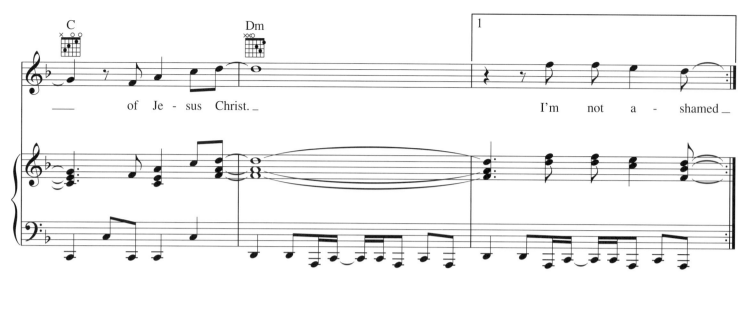

of Je - sus Christ. _____ I'm not a - shamed _____

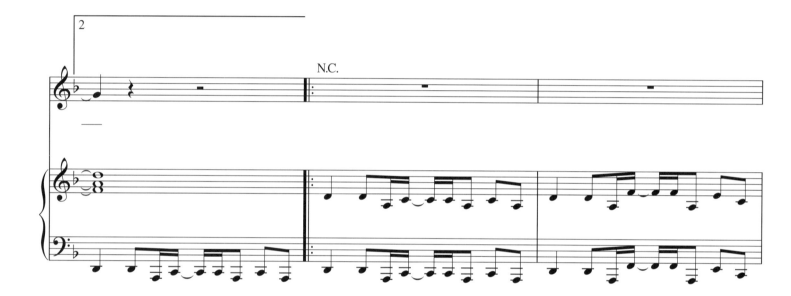

N.C.

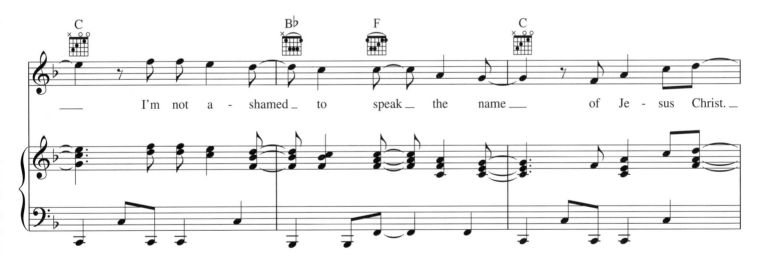

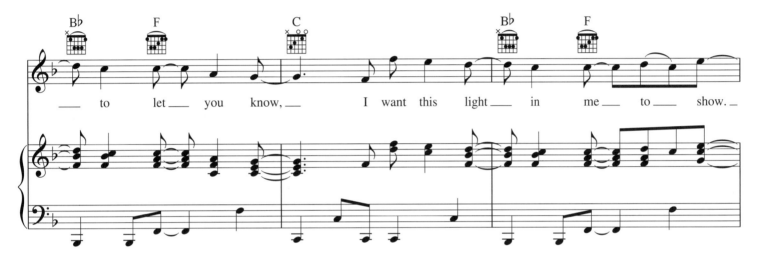

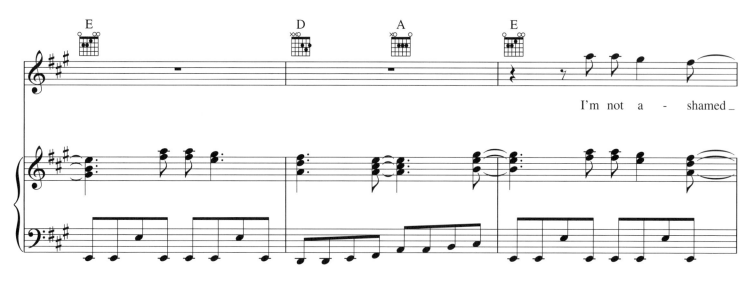

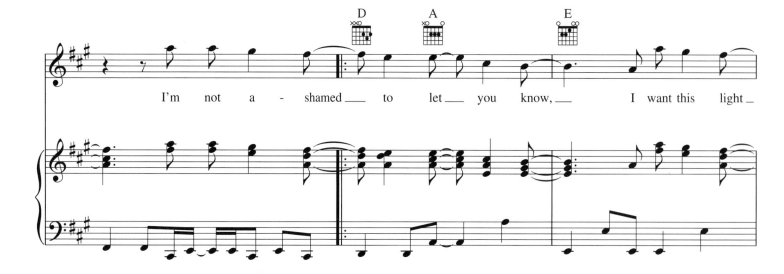

in me to show. I'm not a-shamed to speak the name

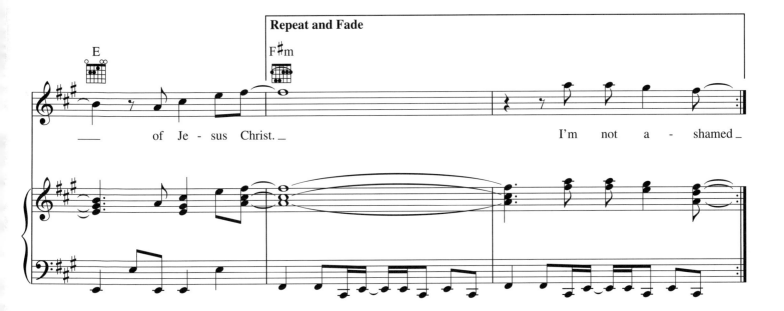

Repeat and Fade

of Je-sus Christ. I'm not a-shamed

Optional Ending

More Contemporary Christian Folios from Hal Leonard

Arranged for Piano, Voice and Guitar

AUDIO ADRENALINE – ADIOS: THE GREATEST HITS

17 of the best from one of the biggest successes in the CCM world. Includes: Big House • Chevette • Get Down • Some Kind of Zombie • Hands and Feet • Never Gonna Be as Big as Jesus • Ocean Floor • We're a Band • and more.

00306825 P/V/G.....................$16.95

THE VERY BEST OF AVALON – TESTIFY TO LOVE

All 16 songs from the 2003 compilation by this acclaimed vocal quartet: Adonai • Can't Live a Day • Don't Save It All for Christmas Day • Everything to Me • Give It Up • Knockin' on Heaven's Door • New Day • Pray • Testify to Love • and more.

00306526 P/V/G.....................$16.95

JEREMY CAMP – BEYOND MEASURE

This CD showcases Camp's powerful voice, which earned him back-to-back Male Vocalist of the Year GMA Music Awards. Our songbook features all 12 tracks, including the hit single "What It Means" and: Beyond Measure • Everything • Give Me Jesus • Let It Fade • Tonight • more.

00306854 P/V/G.....................$16.95

CASTING CROWNS – LIFESONG

11 contemporary rock/worship songs from this popular band's 2005 album. Includes: And Now My Lifesong Sings • Does Anybody Hear Her • Father, Spirit, Jesus • In Me • Lifesong • Love Them like Jesus • Praise You in This Storm • Prodigal • Set Me Free • Stained Glass Masquerade • While You Were Sleeping.

00306748 P/V/G.....................$16.95

THE BEST OF STEVEN CURTIS CHAPMAN

21 songs from this award-winning Contemporary Christian/Gospel legend, including: Dive • The Great Adventure • Heaven in the Real World • Live Out Loud • Magnificent Obsession • More to This Life • No Better Place • Remembering You • and more.

00306811 P/V/G.....................$17.95

DAVID CROWDER BAND COLLECTION

David Crowder's innovative alt-pop style has made him one of today's most popular worship leaders. This collection includes 16 of his best songs: Here Is Our King • No One like You • Open Skies • Our Love Is Loud • You Alone • and more.

00306776 P/V/G.....................$16.95

STEVE GREEN – THE ULTIMATE COLLECTION

25 songs from the hits collection for this gospel star who got his start backing up Sandi Patti and the Gaither Vocal Band in the mid-'70s. Includes: Find Us Faithful • He Is Good • People Need the Lord • We Believe • What Wondrous Love Is This • and more.

00306784 P/V/G.....................$19.95

KUTLESS – STRONG TOWER

The 2005 release by this Christian hard rock band hailing from Oregon includes 13 tracks: We Fall Down • Take Me In • Ready for You • Draw Me Close • Better Is One Day • I Lift My Eyes Up • Word of God Speak • Arms of Love • and more.

00306726 P/V/G.................$16.95

BRIAN LITTRELL – WELCOME HOME

Matching folio to the former Backstreet Boy's solo Contemporary Christian release. Includes all 10 tracks: Angels and Heroes • I'm Alive • My Answer Is You • We Lift You Up • Welcome Home (You) • and more.

00306830 P/V/G...............$16.95

Music Inspired by THE CHRONICLES OF NARNIA

The Lion, The Witch and The Wardrobe 11 songs from the album featuring CCM artists. Includes: I Will Believe (Nichole Nordeman) • Lion (Rebecca St. James) • Remembering You (Steven Curtis Chapman) • Waiting for the World to Fall (Jars of Clay) • and more.

00313311 P/V/G.....................$16.95

NICHOLE NORDEMAN – BRAVE

11 tracks from the 2005 album by this talented singer-songwriter: Brave • Crimson • Gotta Serve Somebody • Hold On • Lay It Down • Live • No More Chains • Real to Me • Someday • We Build • What If.

00306729 P/V/G.................$16.95

PHILLIPS, CRAIG & DEAN – THE ULTIMATE COLLECTION

31 of the greatest hits by this popular CCM trio. Includes: Crucified with Christ • Favorite Song of All • Here I Am to Worship • Lord, Let Your Glory Fall • Midnight Oil • Only You • Restoration • Shine on Us • This Is the Life • The Wonderful Cross • and more.

00306789 P/V/G.....................$19.95

MICHAEL W. SMITH – GREATEST HITS

2ND EDITION

25 of the best songs from this popular Contemporary Christian singer/songwriter, includes: Friends • I Will Be Here for You • Place in This World • Secret Ambition • This Is Your Time • You Are Holy (Prince of Peace) • and more.

00358186 P/V/G.....................$17.95

STARFIELD – BEAUTY IN THE BROKEN

Starfield wrote songs perfect for use in a modern church. Our matching folio to their 2006 release features all 11 tracks: Captivate • Everything Is Beautiful • Great Is the Lord • My Generation • Obsession • Unashamed • and more.

00306832 P/V/G.....................$17.95

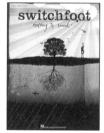

SWITCHFOOT – NOTHING IS SOUND

Switchfoot's rock style and street-smart faith has given them widespread success in CCM and secular arenas. This songbook from their 2005 release features 12 songs: Daisy • Happy Is a Yuppie Word • Lonely Nation • The Setting Sun • Stars • more.

00306756 P/V/G.....................$16.95

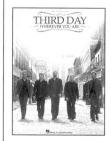

THIRD DAY – WHEREVER YOU ARE

This popular rock band's 2005 release features "Cry Out to Jesus" plus: Carry My Cross • Communion • Eagles • How Do You Know • I Can Feel It • Keep on Shinin' • Love Heals Your Heart • Mountain of God • Rise Up • The Sun Is Shining • Tunnel.

00306766 P/V/G.....................$16.95

CHRIS TOMLIN – ARRIVING

Our matching folio to the 2004 release from this award-winning singer/songwriter and worship leader from Texas features all 11 songs, including the hit singles: Holy Is the Lord • How Great Is Our God • and Indescribable.

00306857 P/V/G...............$16.95